Know-How Philosophy

A Philosophy That Can Improve Itself

By Stanley R. Silver

Union River Research LLC
Owatonna, Minnesota

Know-How Philosophy: A Philosophy That Can Improve Itself
Copyright © 2023 by Stanley R. Silver

All rights reserved. This book or portions thereof may not be reproduced or used without the written permission of the publisher, except for the following special case.

> Because this book is a philosophy book, chapters S23.1 through S23.17 (inclusive) are licensed under a Creative Commons Attribution 4.0 International License (CC BY 4.0). These chapters (and only these chapters) may be reproduced, all or in part, for any use (including commercial and web use, with any amount of editing, translation, or AI modification), *if properly attributed.*
>
> http://creativecommons.org/licenses/by/4.0/deed.en_US

Printed in the United States of America
First Printing March 2023
Revised May 2023
ISBN 978-0-9966543-1-9

Union River Research LLC
Owatonna, MN

www.knowhowphilosophy.com
publisher@knowhowphilosophy.com

Cover Picture - Mosaic of Minerva, located in the Library of Congress Thomas Jefferson Building, Washington, D.C.

Artist - *Elihu Vedder* (1836–1923) American symbolist painter, book illustrator, and poet.

From Wikipedia:

> **Symbolism** was a late 19th-century art movement ... in poetry and other arts seeking to represent absolute truths symbolically through language and metaphorical images...
>
> *https://en.wikipedia.org/wiki/Symbolism_(arts)* *(03/16/2022)*

Exhibit Caption - Pictured on this mosaic in the arched panel is the Roman Goddess Minerva--guardian of civilization. She is portrayed as the Minerva of Peace, but according to the artist who created her, Elihu Vedder (American painter, 1836–1923), the peace and prosperity that she enjoys was attained only through warfare.

A little statue of Nike, a representation of Victory, similar to those erected by ancient Greeks to commemorate their success in battle, stands next to Minerva. The figure is a winged female standing on a globe and holding out a laurel wreath (victory) and palm branch (peace) to the victors.

Shield and Helmet: Although Minerva's shield and helmet have been laid upon the ground, the goddess still holds a long, two-headed spear, showing that she never relaxes her vigilance against the enemies of the country that she protects.

Scroll: Her attention is directed to an unfolded scroll that she holds in her left hand. On this is written a list of various fields of learning, such as Architecture, Law, Statistics, Sociology, Botany, Biography, Mechanics, Philosophy, Zoology, etc. Minerva is therefore also the Goddess of Learning, an activity that can thrive in a peaceful society.

Owl: On Minerva's right is an owl, symbolizing wisdom, perched upon the post of a low parapet.

Inscription: Beneath the mosaic is an inscription from Horace's Ars Poetica: Nil invita Minerva, quae monumentum aere perennius exegit, and translated as, Not unwilling, Minerva raises a monument more lasting than bronze.

This Book's Interpretation – This book interpretates the inscribed quote to mean "Wisdom and learning are the will of Heaven".

Preface

This book is a philosophy book. In it, I present a philosophy of what works, bounded by truth and morality, called know-how philosophy.

Scientists and engineers are trained to set aside judgement in favor of good analysis. Liberal arts graduates are trained to improve judgement using good analysis. Closed-minded people fabricate analysis to justify pre-existing judgement.

Hopefully, this book falls in the liberal arts camp. I tried hard to create a book of informed judgment – personal judgement supported by reason. If some of the ideas presented in this book are used, in turn, to inform readers' judgement, this book will have succeeded.

I dedicate this book to all those who choose good over evil and (at the same time) choose workable over unworkable.

Stan Silver, spring 2023

Prologue

The Road to Wisdom

Trouville – A Lesson with the Rudder
(late 1800s, oil on canvas)

***Paul Jobert** (1863-1942), French painter.*

(Trouville-sur-Mer is a town in Normandy, France)

(Improvement quotes, from past to present.)

The man who moves a mountain begins by carrying away small stones... It does not matter how slowly you go, so long as you do not stop.
Confucius *(551-479 BC), Chinese philosopher.*

For the things we have to learn before we can do them, we learn by doing them.
Aristotle *(384-322 BC), Greek philosopher.*

A wise man will hear, and will increase learning; and a man of understanding shall attain unto wise counsels.
Proverbs 1:5, King James Bible.

When I was a child, I spake as a child, I understood as a child, I thought as a child: but when I became a man, I put away childish things.
1 Corinthians 13:11, King James Bible.

Start by doing what's necessary, then what's possible; and suddenly you are doing the impossible.
Saint Francis of Assisi *(1182-1226), Italian friar and preacher.*

These times are the ancient times, when the world is ancient, and not those which we account ancient *ordine retrogrado*, by a computation backward from ourselves.
Francis Bacon *(1561-1626), English renaissance author, statesman, philosopher.*

If I have seen further... it is by standing upon the shoulders of giants.
Isaac Newton *(1642-1727), English physicist, mathematician.*

The aim of an argument or discussion should not be victory, but progress.
Joseph Joubert (1754-1824), French moralist and essayist.

If I have a thousand ideas and only one turns out to be good, I am satisfied.
Alfred Nobel (1822-1896), Swedish inventor of dynamite.

The secret of getting ahead is getting started. The secret of getting started is breaking your complex overwhelming tasks into small manageable tasks, and then starting on the first one.
Mark Twain (Samuel Langhorne Clemens) (1835-1910), American writer and humorist.

In a moment of decision, the best thing you can do is the right thing to do, the next best thing is the wrong thing, and the worst thing you can do is nothing.
Theodore Roosevelt (1858-1919), American politician, naturalist, and writer.

Truth in our ideas means their power to work.
William James (1842-1910), American philosopher.

Whether you think you can, or you think you can't – you're right.
Henry Ford (1863-1947), American industrialist.

There are some things which cannot be learned quickly, and time, which is all we have, must be paid heavily for their acquiring. They are the very simplest things and because it takes a man's life to know them the little new that each man gets from life is very costly and the only heritage he has to leave.
Ernest Hemingway (1899-1961), American author.

The way to get good ideas is to get lots of ideas, and throw the bad ones away.
Linus Pauling *(1901-1994), American chemist and biologist.*

The road to wisdom?
Well, it's plain and simple to express:
Err and err and err again
But less and less and less.
Piet Hein *(1905-1996), Danish inventor, poet.*

All models are wrong, but some are useful.
George E. P. Box *(1919-2013), British born American statistician.*

Introduction

The Alchymist, in Search of the Philosopher's Stone
(1771, oil on canvas)

Joseph Wright of Derby (1734-1797), English painter.

"The search for truth" is a philosophical phrase that has served mankind well for millennia. Until recently, this phrase seems to have meant "the search for that which makes us better", rather than a search for some logical construct. It implied a collective attempt at the continuous improvement of mankind.

In the past four hundred years, science has grown increasingly influential. Especially since Darwin published "On the Origin of Species", the power of science has touched all aspects of our lives.

This includes philosophy. Science has encroached on philosophy in two ways. The first and obvious way is that a large chunk of natural philosophy "broke off" and became science. The second and not-so-obvious way is that the success of scientific "truth" has begun to interfere with the meaning of the philosophical phrase "the search for truth".

Scientists and engineers are taught to *set aside* their judgement in favor of careful analysis. Liberal arts graduates are taught to *improve* their judgement using careful analysis.

We *do not want* the shielding of a nuclear reactor, the thickness of an airplane's wings, or the strength of a bridge's supports to be determined by partial evidence, logical thinking, experience, and gut feeling. Instead, we want full evidence, logical thinking, and no gut feeling to be used.

We *do want* military attack plans, business expansion decisions, and political compromises to be made using partial evidence, logical thinking, experience, and gut feeling. In other words, **informed judgement**. This is because there *is no better way* – there never can be or will be full evidence.

To a scientist, "truth" is that which is proven by evidence. To a liberal arts graduate, "truth" is that which best guides our judgement.

This disparity did not matter when liberal arts graduates dominated the world outside of laboratories – their meaning of "the search for truth" prevailed, and for better or worse, informed judgement was used to make decisions.

Now that liberal arts graduates share power equally with scientists and engineers, this conflict of meaning is causing genuine confusion in decision making.

The tension between hard evidence and judgement is especially acute in modern philosophy – more specifically, in the direction modern philosophy should take to move forward. For example, should we discard the fable "The boy who cried wolf", or the folk saying "The pot calling the kettle black" because there is no historical evidence they ever occurred?

This book attempts to address this tension in modern philosophy by approaching philosophy as a three-part search:

- a search for empirical truth,
- a search for what is morally right, and
- a search for what works (constrained by empirical truth and morality).

This three-part approach to philosophy, however, is not the topic of this book. Rather, the topic of this book is the field that this three-part approach calls attention to – the philosophy of what works, or, as it is called by this book, know-how philosophy.

By exploring and expanding know-how philosophy, this book hopes to contribute in some small way to the steady progress of philosophy, and, in turn, to the steady progress of mankind – the desired outcome of good philosophy.

Three Types of Philosophy

The School of Athens
(1511, fresco)

Raffaello Sanzio *(1483-1520), Italian painter, architect.*

The invention of scientific consensus means one scientist can answer a scientific question for all of us – we don't each have to reinvent the wheel.

Philosophy, on the other hand, is the study of questions that cannot be answered by one person for the rest of us. Specifically, it is the study of questions that have a single answer that matters, but a single answer which we must *each find for ourselves*.

Three types

There are many ways to divide philosophy. This book divides philosophy into three broad types – **natural philosophy**, **moral philosophy**, and **know-how philosophy**.

Natural philosophy asks whether hypotheses are *true or false*. Moral philosophy asks whether actions are *right or wrong*. Know-how philosophy asks whether action A works *better or worse* than action B.

Tax evasion sometimes works. Safe-cracking sometimes works. Know-how philosophy without morality is amoral Machiavellianism, adherents of which will (to be polite) not end up in Heaven. However, by separating moral and know-how philosophy into sibling philosophies, know-how philosophy can be constrained by, but separate from, morality.

Likewise, with natural philosophy as a sibling, know-how philosophy can be constrained by, but separate from, justification and proof. Without intrinsic justification and proof, know-how philosophy gives up the benefits of *consensus*, but gains in return the benefits of *subjectivity*.

One of the benefits of subjectivity is *simplicity*. A know-how philosophy is merely a collection of what works for a single person.

Hectosophy

To use with know-how philosophy, this book proposes a new tool – a new writing form – a new way to write subjective philosophy on paper.

The proposed writing form is called the **hectosophy**, from the Greek *hecto* meaning *hundred*, and *sophy* meaning *knowledge or wisdom*.

A hectosophy is a collection of named ideas that is limited to one hundred items. To add a new idea to the collection after this size is reached, an old idea must be discarded. This causes the list of ideas to grow in quality, not quantity.

As a *ratchet* for collecting ever-better subjective ideas, and as a container for *sharing* subjective ideas, the hectosophy can be:

- an alternative to the *essay*, in that it can prevent the lock-in that may come from compressing a set of ideas into a single concept, and
- an extension of the *personal journal* in that it can separate the wheat from the chaff – the message from the noise.

Second Introduction

To be precise, this is the hectosophy's second introduction. The hectosophy was also presented in the author's first book, called *Accumulism, A Philosophy of Learning*, published in 2016.

Influence

The idea of the hectosophy was directly and heavily influenced by the *pattern language* writing form of Austrian-born British-American architect and design theorist **Christopher Alexander** (1936 – 2022).

It was also directly and heavily influenced by the writing form of the first wiki – called the *wiki wiki web* – which was developed by American computer programmer **Ward Cunningham** (1949 –).

Both of these writing forms were designed to record wisdom (albeit consensus wisdom), using collections of named discrete ideas.

Stripped to its very essence, this book adds *subjectivity* and *fixed-size lists* to the work of Alexander and Cunningham.

Similarity

Although this book was not directly influenced by German philosopher **Friedrich Nietzsche** (1844 - 1900), or the philosophy of **pragmatism**, hectosophies share similarities to Nietzsche's aphoristic style of philosophy, and this book's search for what works is related to one of the tenets of pragmatism – "Truth in our ideas means their power to work".

In summary

A ***know-how philosophy*** (countable noun) is defined as *a personal and subjective collection of what works, usually recorded as a hectosophy, that is constrained by, but separate from, truth and morality.*

The ***field*** of know-how philosophy (uncountable noun) is defined as the *study* of such philosophies.

Benefits of subjective philosophy

- As stated above, a subjective philosophy is *simple*. It is a collection of what works for a single person.

- A subjective philosophy can model human systems using an arbitrary number of artificial divisions. Seven habits of highly effective people, three types of philosophy (as defined by this book), sixteen Myers Briggs types, and many other numbered sets are subjective. Science reflects reality, but for many cases, reality is too complex to be useful. *Artificial-division models* sacrifice some reality for an approximation that is simple enough to use, but still predictive enough to be useful.

- A subjective philosophy can contain hunches, unexplained correlations, and partial ideas. Recording *half-formed wisdom* is necessary when addressing problems that are too hard to solve in a single cognitive leap. For example, this book contains many half-formed ideas that will wither on the vine, and hopefully some half-formed ideas that will be found useful and later extended.

Benefits of hectosophies

- Comparing hectosophies side-by-side gives the benefit that single ideas can be swapped without the need to fully accept or fully reject the complete philosophy of an author. In other words, the *atomic unit* of know-how philosophy can be the *idea*, and not the *author*.

- Once the idea becomes the unit of philosophy instead of the author, philosophies can be constructed using *interchangeable parts*.

- Most importantly, hectosophies give know-how philosophy the benefit of being able to *improve itself*, without the need of consensus. If a single person collects what works about collecting what works, and records it in a hectosophy, then that person is, by definition, using know-how philosophy to improve know-how philosophy.

Culling hectosophies in practice

Theoretically, removing one old idea each time one new idea is added to a hectosophy will result in a list of ideas that continually improves in quality. In practice, hectosophies are always culled in batches. One hundred twenty ideas are collected, then the list is culled to a size of one hundred. Twenty more ideas are collected, then the list is again culled to a size of one hundred.

This is necessary because, over time, existing ideas in the list become more "weighty", while new ideas continue to be small. Eventually, twenty new small ideas will add one or two new "weighty" ideas to the hectosophy when the combined ideas are culled.

For example, one of the author's hectosophies is kept in a journal with twenty-five lines per page. The hectosophy comprises one page for existing ideas, and one page for new ideas. Each time a total of two pages of ideas are attained (fifty ideas), the list is culled to one page of ideas (twenty-five ideas).

Splicing ideas

Borrowing a word from the vocabulary of sailing ships and the movie industry (when movies were recorded on film), *splicing* is defined as

- *adding ideas to a hectosophy*, or
- *combining two or more hectosophies into one hectosophy.*

Example: an original idea is spliced into a hectosophy – the idea is added and then the hectosophy is culled.

Example: two ideas from hectosophy B are spliced into hectosophy A – the ideas are added to hectosophy A and then hectosophy A is culled.

Example: three hectosophies of one hundred ideas each are spliced – the top one hundred ideas from all the hectosophies are combined into one new hectosophy.

A person improves their own hectosophies by splicing original ideas and splicing ideas from others' hectosophies.

Examples of know-how philosophies

Sun Tzu's *The Art of War*, *The Analects of Confucius*, and the *Tao Te Ching* are know-how philosophies (that do not use hectosophies). Commonplace books (also known as commonplaces) are know-how philosophies. A collection of best practices is a know-how philosophy. This book is a know-how philosophy.

https://en.wikipedia.org/wiki/Commonplace_book (02/11/2023)

In summary (again)

Know-how philosophy (uncountable noun, using hectosophies):

- can model human systems with a useful number of artificial divisions,
- supports half-formed wisdom,
- allows the idea to be the atomic unit of philosophy rather than the author,
- allows philosophies to be built from interchangeable parts, and
- can improve itself without consensus.

Know-How Improvement

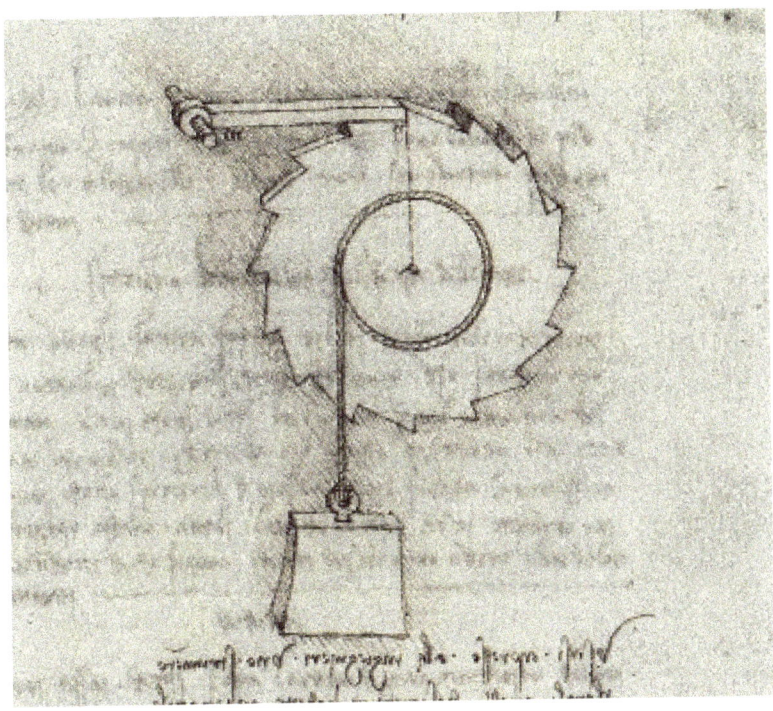

Ratchet and pawl mechanism, *Codex Madrid I*, page 117r (1490's, manuscript illustration)

Leonardo Da Vinci *(1452-1519), Italian painter, sculptor, scientist.*

Speaking of artificial divisions, hectosophies can be used for five types of know-how improvement:

- improving understanding,
- improving skills,
- improving rule-based processes,
- improving complex skills, and
- improving self-improvement.

Improving understanding

To use a hectosophy to improve subjective understanding:

- Set a goal of what you want to understand.
- Use trial and error to collect a list of ideas related to your goal.
- Occasionally cull the list, keeping the top one hundred ideas.

The one hundred ideas in your list will collectively form an ever-improving holistic model of what you are trying to understand.

The terms *improving understanding, improving a mental model*, and *improving a model* are used interchangeably in this book.

Examples of hectosophies used for understanding are hectosophies titled "How are instincts stored in DNA?", "How is wealth created?", and "What are good forms of government?".

Improving skills

To use a hectosophy to improve a skill:

- Set a goal of the skill you want to improve.
- Practice the skill.

- Collect what works in a list. In other words, collect best practices.
- Occasionally cull the list, keeping the top one hundred practices.
- Here is the non-intuitive part – after you collect best practices, do not follow them (completely). If you always follow best practices, you will not try anything new, and you will stop learning.
- Rather, for repetitive skills that you want to continually improve, do each iteration of the skill differently for the rest of your life.

The one hundred practices in your list will act (metaphorically) as an ever-improving toolset, or quiver of arrows, from which to draw as needed when practicing the skill.

Examples of such hectosophies are hectosophies titled "Hiking in upstate New York", "Programming with JavaScript", and "Shoeing a horse".

Improving rule-based processes

A collection of rules can be defined in such a way that following the explicit rules results in an implicit process.

For example, a company often has a set of discrete rules for software development, which, when followed, result in an implicit software development process.

To use a hectosophy to improve a rule-based process:

- Set a goal of the process that you want to improve.
- Use trial and error to collect rules that, when followed, result in the desired implicit process.
- One hundred rules is usually too many – implicit processes often use five, ten, or twenty rules.

- Occasionally cull the list, keeping the top (five, ten, or twenty) rules.

Examples of such hectosophies are hectosophies titled "Agile programming", and "Morning routine".

Improving complex skills

A complex skill has several components. To use hectosophies to improve a complex skill:

- Divide the complex skill into subskills, sub-understandings, and sub-processes.
- Each subskill, sub-understanding, and sub-process becomes a single *axis of improvement*.
- For each axis of improvement, create one hectosophy.
- The pursued axes of improvement of a complex skill will change as you improve. In fact, discovering ever-better axes of improvement is part of learning a complex skill.

A *hectosophy ark* is defined as a collection of named hectosophies – named axes of improvement – used to capture a complex skill on paper and subsequently improve it.

Ark is an archaic English word derived from the Latin word arca, meaning "chest, box, or coffer". The word is commonly known from the Christian Bible, in which there are two arks – a box-like boat, and a container that held the ten commandments.

A hectosophy ark can be thought of as a fixed-size box of hectosophies for ratcheting and sharing ideas.

A hectosophy ark will act as an ever-improving collection of models, toolsets, and processes to use when practicing a complex skill.

Both the content of an ark and the axes of improvement of an ark will improve as wisdom is gained. With better axes of improvement, wisdom will be gained faster. Thus, when using a hectosophy ark, learning gradually accelerates.

Arks are recursive. An ark can contain sub-arks in addition to hectosophies.

Just as a two hectosophies can be compared side-by-side and ideas exchanged, two hectosophy arks can be compared side-by-side and ideas exchanged. Both hectosophies and hectosophy arks allow ideas to be the unit of philosophy (instead of authors) and allow philosophies to be manufactured from interchangeable parts.

Examples of hectosophy arks are arks titled: "Doing well at work", and "Starting a real estate business". This book is a hectosophy ark.

Improving self-improvement
On the one hand, self-improvement is a complex skill. Like other complex skills, self-improvement can be improved using a hectosophy ark.

On the other hand, self-improvement and know-how improvement are *special* complex skills. Thus, the following two special arks are defined.

A **meta-ark** is defined as *a hectosophy ark that contains one person's self-improvement philosophy (countable noun) and know-how philosophy (countable noun).*

A **private-improvement ark** is defined as *a hectosophy ark that contains one person's day-to-day self-improvement progress.*

A private-improvement ark puts into practice the theory contained in a meta-ark.

Each know-how philosophy practitioner will benefit by having one meta-ark and one private-improvement ark. Meta-arks are to be shared, and private-improvement arks are to be kept private.

As meta-arks are shared, and original ideas and ideas from others' meta-arks are spliced, each person's self-improvement philosophy and know-how philosophy will gradually improve.

As individual meta-arks improve, humanity's collective know-how philosophy (uncountable noun) will hopefully also improve.

Meta-Ark

Solomon Before the Ark of the Covenant
(1747, oil on canvas)

Blaise Nicholas Le Sueur *(1716–1783), German painter and engraver of allegorical and historical subjects.*

A personal meta-ark

The remaining chapters of this book contain the author's meta-ark for the year 2023. The ark is named **Meta-Ark Silver 23** (S23 for short).

S23 comprises 16 axes of improvement – 16 hectosophies – plus a summary, presented one per chapter. Some hectosophies are lists of ideas, some are in question-and-answer format, some are prose, and some are prose with numbered summaries.

The hope is that all those who construct a meta-ark with a similar structure – with axes of improvement similar to those of S23 – will be able to swap ideas and learn fast from each other.

Mostly borrowed ideas

A few ideas in S23 are original. A few ideas are copied verbatim from others (and attributed). Most of the ideas in S23 are known learning and improvement ideas that are reworded (and unattributed).

The main contribution that S23 attempts to make is not its unoriginal content, but its original structure – the way it assembles known ideas – the fact that it is *itself* a hectosophy ark.

Religious substitution

As everyone should, the author believes his own religion is the best religion. Therefore, religious examples in S23 are drawn from the author's own religion.

Each reader of S23 should believe *their own* religion is the best. To gain the most from S23, each reader should substitute their own religion (or religion alternative) into S23 in place of the author's religion.

A snapshot of wisdom and maturity

The goal of a meta-ark is not to be wise and mature. The goal of a meta-ark is to accurately capture the current wisdom and maturity of its author.

If this is done well, a meta-ark will appear to others as partly wise and partly sophomoric. This is as it should be. Hopefully meta-ark readers know enough to splice good ideas and ignore everything else.

Meta-Ark Silver 23 (S23)

Axes of Improvement

Acquiring wisdom
    S23.1 – Know-How Philosophy

Becoming an adult
    S23.2 – Moral Philosophy
    S23.3 – Free Will
    S23.4 – Western Liberal Arts Education
    S23.5 – Conform to Team Culture
    S23.6 – Love Your Enemies

Improving as an adult
    S23.7 – Self-Improvement
    S23.8 – Mnemonics

Improving as a team
    S23.9 – Co-Improvement
    S23.10 – Agile Agile Programming

Understanding synergy
    S23.11 – Synergy
    S23.12 – The Evolution of Evolution
    S23.13 – Team Worth
    S23.14 – Religion
    S23.15 – Social Structure

Further thoughts
    S23.16 – Collecting Seashells

And
    S23.17 – Summary

S23.1 – Know-How Philosophy

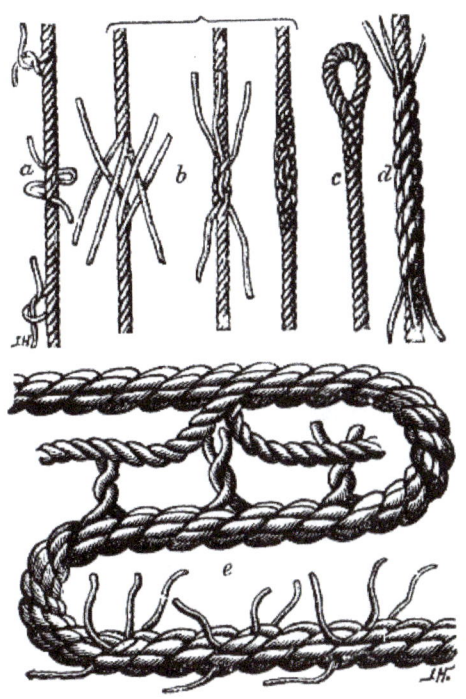

An image from *Nordisk Familjebok*
(a Swedish Encyclopedia, published between 1876 and 1926)

Entry: "Splits"
(English Translation: "Splice")

http://runeberg.org/nfcf/0424.html (1/22/2023)

- *Philosophy* is the study of those questions that have a single answer – a single answer, however, which we must each find for ourselves.

- There is **consensus of action** in philosophy. When a nation is formed, a law is passed, or a court judgement is made, philosophical agreement is reached. There is **personal empiricism** – personal judgement is influenced by what works for an individual. **Reason** is at the heart of philosophy. But there is **no universal consensus** in philosophy – no universal empirical proof or logical proof as there is in science and math.

- The fact that there are universal single answers, but no universal proof of those single answers, makes philosophy intriguing and challenging.

- S23 divides philosophy into three main types. **Natural philosophy** asks whether hypotheses are *true or false*. **Moral philosophy** asks whether actions are *right or wrong*. **Know-how philosophy** asks whether action A works *better or worse* than action B.

- A know-how philosophy (countable noun) is defined as *a personal and subjective collection of what works, usually recorded as a hectosophy, that is constrained by, but separate from, truth and morality.*

- The field of know-how philosophy (uncountable noun) is defined as the *study* of such philosophies, and *how to improve them.*

- A *hectosophy* is a subjective fixed-length list of what works. Hectosophies originated by adding *subjectivity* and a *fixed length* to the pattern language work of American architect and design theorist **Christopher Alexander** (1936 – 2022) and American computer programmer **Ward Cunningham** (1949 –).

- Hectosophies are good for the improvement of understanding, skills, and rule-based processes.

- A *hectosophy ark* is a fixed-size collection of named hectosophies. The named hectosophies represent axes of improvement. Hectosophy arks are good for improving complex skills (comprising sub-understanding, sub-skills, sub-processes, and sub-arks).

- A *meta-ark* contains one person's combined know-how philosophy (countable noun) and self-improvement philosophy (countable noun). Meta-arks are designed to be shown to friends, so that ideas can be swapped.

- A *private-improvement ark* contains one person's day-to-day self-improvement progress. A private-improvement ark puts into practice the theory contained in a meta-ark and is usually kept private.

- It is assumed that each know-how philosophy practitioner will have one meta-ark and one private-improvement ark.

- Each person improves their meta-ark by splicing original ideas and splicing ideas from others' arks.

- As each person's meta-ark improves, it is hoped that humanity's know-how philosophy (uncountable noun) and self-improvement philosophy (uncountable noun) will collectively improve.

S23.2 – Moral Philosophy

Saint Thomas Aquinas
(1476, tempera, poplar panel)

Carlo Crivelli *(1435-1495), Italian Renaissance painter.*

Free individuals voluntarily give up some of their freedom to society – to family, to community, and to a sovereign state. In return, individuals gain the benefits of society and state, including protection for the freedoms they retain.

Wrong is defined as *that set of freedoms – of rights – individuals must give up for society to function.*

For society to function, individuals must give up (among other things) murder, stealing, lying under oath, and disobeying the law. Hence, murder, stealing, lying under oath, and disobeying the law are wrong.

Morality is not subjective. It is external to the self and absolute. For society to function, all citizens must give up the same personal freedoms and are therefore bound by the same code of what is right and wrong.

Although morality is absolute, each citizen's view of morality differs by a small amount. Therefore, real-world societies reach consensus on what *behaviors* to allow and not allow, instead of trying to reach consensus on *morality* itself.

Moral philosophy is the study of:

- What is right and wrong – what freedoms must be given up for society to function, and what freedoms are retained by individuals.
- How humans pass on what is right and wrong from parent to child.
- How societies reconcile personal viewpoints of absolute morality to reach consensus on allowed behavior.
- How societies control "cheaters" – those that transgress right and wrong – that transgress society's moral code.

S23.3 – Free Will

Transitioning from Child to Adult

Portrait of Erasmus of Rotterdam
(1523, oil on wood)

Hans Holbein the Younger *(1497-1543), German-Swiss painter and printmaker.*

Some thoughts on free will

- Human societies work best when adults are free and responsible. Being a free and responsible adult means:

    - asserting free will,
    - using your free will to take responsibility for yourself,
    - choosing good over evil (accepting God, or some equivalent),
    - choosing what works over what does not work (accepting and respecting science and good judgment), and
    - voluntarily surrendering some of your personal freedom in the form of duty to society and a sovereign state.

    (Depending on culture and religion, different peoples of the world give up different amounts of personal freedom in return for different amounts of benefit and protection from their sovereign state.)

- A responsible adult chooses to steadily improve being a responsible adult.

- To this end, keeping a journal is helpful. Or perhaps some other symbol or ritual that shows that you are now in charge of yourself.

- Being an adult is fundamentally different than being a child:

    - The way a parent treats a child is not the way an adult should treat another adult. Rather, the way an adult treats a child is more like the way an adult should treat themselves once they are grown.

- Parents mold their children. Adults accept other adults as they currently are.
- Consequently, an adult cannot copy the way they were treated by their parents while they were growing up (except when raising their own children). In other words, they cannot mold other adults. An adult must somehow learn to treat adults as adults by some other means.

- For a child, there is external empirical truth, external morality, and *external judgement* (the judgement of the parent).

- For an adult, there is external empirical truth, external morality, and *internal judgement* (which replaces the judgement of the parent).

An adult still needs to believe in a single right way, but it is a single right way they must *choose for themselves*.

- This choice of a single right way cannot be a coin toss. It must be an honest best choice.

- ***Informed judgement*** – making honest best choices – is improved through use, as a muscle is.

- If the switch to free will is not made – if an adult clings to the childish notion there is external truth in all areas, so that informed judgement is not needed – then good judgement will not develop.

- Likewise, if an adult takes freedom too far – if an adult believes that all choices are equal, so that there is no difference between whims and honest best choices – then good judgement will not develop.

Blame game

- Assigning blame to an adult is different than assigning blame to a child.

- When a child is to blame for something wrong, it is the parent's job to see that the child takes responsibility and fixes things.

- When another adult is to blame for something wrong *and they apologize*, this is a signal they are taking responsibility and will proceed to fix it (they were taught well as a child).

- When another adult is to blame for something wrong *and they do not apologize*, you should not expect that adult to fix things. If you want that something fixed, it is *your* responsibility to see that it is fixed.

- A criminal is not responsible for catching himself and putting himself in jail. An attacking general is not responsible for defeating herself. If you call someone a jerk, you cannot then expect that person to fix their wrongs – a jerk, by definition, is someone who does not *care* about offending others.

- When an adult is to blame for something, often it is for something they have done on purpose or something they have done from ignorance. In the first case they will not want to fix it and in the second case they will not know how to fix it.

Driving the bus

The following metaphor is informative.

- When it comes to human nature, you can jump in front of the bus, you can ride the bus, or you can drive the bus.

- If you attempt something that goes against human nature, you will not succeed. You are jumping in front of the bus, and you will be squashed.

- If you give in to basic animal instinct, you are riding the bus. You have no control over your destination.

- If, however, you guide human nature, without directly opposing it, you are driving the bus. The *rational you* acknowledges, understands, and works with human nature for the benefit of you and others.

- Opposing human nature or giving in to animal instinct feels good but strips you of power. Choosing to guide human nature (your own and others'), though more difficult, gives you power.

S23.4 – Western Liberal Arts Education

Allegory of the Seven Liberal Arts
(1590, oil on oak wood)

***Maerten de Vos** (1532 – 1603), Flemish painter.*

From Wikipedia:

> **Liberal arts education** (from Latin liberalis "free" and ars "art or principled practice") is the traditional academic program in Western higher education. Liberal arts takes the term art in the sense of a learned skill rather than specifically the fine arts.
>
> https://en.wikipedia.org/wiki/Liberal_arts_education
> (4/6/2022)

What is the purpose of a liberal arts education?

The purpose is twofold:

1) Turn a student into an adult who can make difficult decisions that balance competing forces and are based on free will, morals, and principles.

2) Give the aspiring adult an understanding of human nature that can be used to predict individual and group behavior, so the difficult decisions made by the adult produce the outcomes desired by the adult.

How are students turned into adults?

Students are turned into adults by exposing them to many ideas, requiring them to choose the ideas they believe are right, and then challenging that choice and requiring the aspiring adult to defend it. Repeatedly. This approach is called *Socratic inquiry* or the *Socratic method*.

How are aspiring adults given an understanding of human nature?

Students can be trained to make adult decisions by requiring them to defend choices of any type. For example, medical residency is a growing-up program where new doctors are required to defend medical choices. Army basic training is a growing-up program whose aim is good battlefield decisions.

Liberal arts education for the most part requires aspiring adults to defend choices of ideas gleaned from the classics – the great books of history. These classics discuss human behavior and what it means to be a responsible adult. Thus, aspiring adults are *taught* models of human behavior and being an adult from the great books at the same time they are being *trained* to make adult decisions.

How old is Western liberal arts education?

European universities date from the founding of the University of Bologna in 1088 or the University of Paris (c. 1150–70). In round numbers this is one thousand years ago. If we consider the similarities of a liberal arts education to Roman and Greek education, we can say this system of education is 2400 years old.

Has liberal arts education steadily improved during this time?

As human knowledge expanded, liberal arts education incorporated the expanded knowledge. But the techniques of teaching and training for the most part stayed the same.

What are the strengths of liberal arts education (in general)?

Each year, a large group of new adults is minted who can accurately predict individual and group human behavior and make good decisions based on their predictions.

What are the weaknesses of liberal arts education (in general)?

The fact that it has lasted for so long means that for all practical purposes there are no internal weaknesses of liberal arts education. Perhaps the biggest external weakness is that the modern success of science risks obscuring the difference between scientific truth and informed judgement.

If enough people confuse scientific truth and liberal-arts-trained judgement, perhaps the institution will suffer. In the short term.

In the long term, adults with a good understanding of human nature tend to be the ones who win.

What about the thesis of Alan Bloom, that the minds of American students are "closing"?

American philosopher, classicist, and academician **Alan Bloom** (1930 – 1992), in his book *The Closing of the American Mind*, presents the opinion that the advent of "cultural relativism", which superficially seems to encourage open-mindedness, actually closes student's minds to new ideas.

Bloom writes:

> … Prejudices, strong prejudices, are visions about the way things are… Error is indeed our enemy, but it alone points to the truth and therefore deserves our respectful treatment. The mind that has no prejudices at the outset is empty.
>
> https://en.wikipedia.org/wiki/The_Closing_of_the_American_Mind (05/22/2022)

In a nutshell, he seems to be saying that if all ideas are equal – if students do not believe there is *only one answer*, then there is no need to improve your own ideas, and even if you wanted to improve your own ideas, how would you define better?

What is S23's opinion of Bloom's thesis?

S23 *rejects* Bloom's pessimism. Socrates, the "patron saint" of philosophy, was sentenced to death for corrupting the minds of Athens's youth. Every single generation since then has lamented the state of their own youth. It is either very ironic or very understandable that a professor with deep knowledge of the classics would claim that today's students are regressing.

S23 *supports* Bloom's view that each student should *take a stand* – should form a working model – as the first step of a *never-ending search for a single answer*. S23 restates Blooms search for truth as a three-part search:

- a search for empirical truth,
- a search for morality, and
- a search for what works (constrained by empirical truth and morality).

Each student should also believe that the stand they take, while not the *final* answer, is *currently* the best single answer. In other words, each student should **trust their own judgment** (while keeping an open mind).

If three students answer a philosophical question differently, each student should believe **their answer is right**, while respecting the others' answers as *right, but less right*.

Should we agree?

- *Consensus* is a friend of joint action.

- *Respectful competition of ideas* is a friend of philosophy and liberal arts education.

- *Ambivalence* is a friend of nobody.

S23.5 – Conform to Team Culture

The Tribute Money
(1612, oil on panel)

***Peter Paul Rubens** (1577 – 1640), Flemish artist.*

Render therefore unto Caesar the things which are Caesar's; and unto God the things that are God's.

Mathew 20:21, King James Bible

Improving Teams

A parent gently points out mistakes that a child makes and helps the child fix them. Therefore, growing up, children form a mindset of improvement – of seeing and fixing mistakes.

When joining an adult team, this mindset must by repressed (or, at the very least, carefully channeled).

The simple adult rule for improving teams is:

> *Don't.*

The purpose of an adult team is to take advantage of the synergy that comes from the division of labor. Twenty people acting together are more powerful and more productive than twenty people acting alone.

A team works best when each person does their own job well. If one person of a team changes, the smooth functioning of a team can suffer. For example, if a person who regularly produces ten widgets an hour starts producing eleven, or producing nine, it can negatively affect the team.

Conforming to teams

A more refined adult rule for improving teams is:

> *Conform to team culture.*

Improvement is helpful if it is part of team culture. Good team owners and managers create a team culture that includes continuous improvement.

Struggling against team culture to attempt improvement is counterproductive.

A team member should continuously improve toward doing their assigned duty well. They should do team improvement that is part of their assigned duty. They should do team improvement that is part of team culture. Period.

Conform to go fast

Conforming to team culture is not a burden. It is not an end goal. It is a means to an end – an approach that allows you to be productive and learn fast.

Outside of duty (which means conforming to teams you are *obliged* to belong to), to gain the most benefit from conforming to team culture:

- choose to belong to (and conform to) ***doing teams*** on which you are *productive*, and
- choose to belong to (and conform to) ***very small learning teams*** on which you *learn fast*.

Gradually remove yourself from teams whose culture does not benefit you.

If you are an owner or a manager, build a team culture that includes improvement.

Dangers of conformity

If you let conforming to a team influence your life outside that team – if you conform *as a person*, and not just *as a team member* – then conformity is not good.

On the other hand, pretending to conform to team culture is not good either.

Keep your independence, and use free will to genuinely conform to team culture when you are with a team.

Conforming does not mean compromising values

You must not compromise values to conform to a team. If you cannot conform to God's word and a team at the same time, do not be part of the team.

S23.6 – Love Your Enemies

What Our Lord Saw from the Cross
(1894, watercolor)

James Tissot *(1836 – 1902), French painter and illustrator.*

But I say unto you, Love your enemies, bless them that curse you, do good to them that hate you, and pray for them which despitefully use you, and persecute you;

Mathew 5:44, King James Bible

Then said Jesus, Father, forgive them; for they know not what they do.

Luke 23:34, King James Bible

Love all, like some

Liking everyone as an adult – or even getting along with everyone – goes against human nature and will eventually fail. As an adult, you will and should dislike some people, and you will and should be disliked by some people.

Hating those you dislike, however, is giving in to animal instinct. It feels good but leaves you powerless.

Choosing to love and forgive your enemies is neither opposing human nature nor giving in to animal instinct. It is choosing to guide human nature for your own and others' benefit.

Hate the sin, love the sinner.

The following excerpts are from a sermon titled "Loving Your Enemies" by American minister and civil rights leader **Martin Luther King Jr.** (1929 – 1968). S23 suggests you read the whole sermon:

> …In the fifth chapter of the gospel as recorded by Saint Matthew, we read these very arresting words flowing from the lips of our Lord and Master: "Ye have heard that it has been said, 'Thou shall love thy neighbor, and hate thine enemy.' But I say unto you, Love your enemies, bless them that curse you, do good to them that hate you, and pray for them that despitefully use you; that ye may be the children of your Father which is in heaven."

> …Far from being the pious injunction of a utopian dreamer, this command is an absolute necessity for the survival of our civilization. Yes, it is love that will save our world and our civilization, love even for enemies.

> …If I hit you and you hit me and I hit you back and you hit me back and go on, you see, that goes on ad

infinitum. It just never ends. Somewhere somebody must have a little sense, and that's the strong person. The strong person is the person who can cut off the chain of hate, the chain of evil.

https://kinginstitute.stanford.edu/king-papers/documents/loving-your-enemies-sermon-delivered-dexter-avenue-baptist-church (12/6/2022)

S23.7 – Self-Improvement

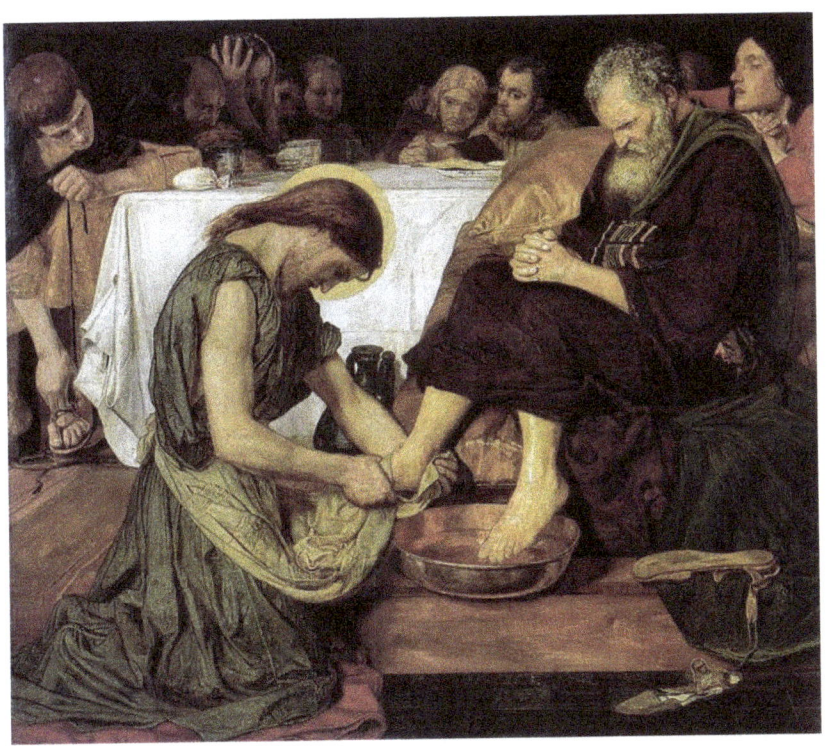

Jesus Washing Peter's Feet
(1856, oil on canvas)

Ford Madox Brown (1821 – 1893), British painter of moral and historical subjects.

Five levels of self-improvement

Self-improvement can be divided into five levels, which are best mastered in order.

Level 1: Know-How Improvement
Level 2: Harmony
Level 3: Learning From All
Level 4: Habit Improvement
Level 5: Goal-Driven Improvement

If you attempt Level 5 goal-driven improvement without first mastering the other four levels, you will end up fighting yourself. Fighting yourself makes change "hard".

=== Level 1 === Know-How Improvement ===

Know-how improvement is addressed in chapter S23.1.

*Once you have **started a journal**, **seeded your own meta-ark**, and started a **private-improvement ark** – in other words, once you have started steady know-how improvement – you are ready for Level 2.*

=== Level 2 === Harmony ===

Good and bad struggle

Struggle is necessary. A person who never struggles is weak. However, like cholesterol, there is **good struggle** and **bad struggle**. Struggling *against* the world is bad, while struggling *along with* the world is good.

Harmony means not struggling *against* the world.

Level 2 self-improvement involves converting bad struggle to good struggle. In other words, first moving toward harmony, then moving toward working hard.

Reducing bad struggle

Western religion, Eastern religion (especially), and many secular philosophies describe effective ways to reduce struggle against the world. S23 uses the wording of Western religion.

Serving God

Western religion teaches that God is served through ***morality*** (not doing wrong) and ***harmony*** (not struggling against the world).

Harmony is achieved by ***humbly serving others*** while ***mastering ourselves***. By being (in secular terms) a self-motivated team player.

Harmony 1 – humbly serving others

When we are with others, God is served (indirectly) by humbly serving those others. This is done by:

- conforming to team culture,
- cooperating with cooperative people and respectfully competing with competitive people,
- moving to better teams as needed, and
- standing up to, but forgiving, those who oppose you.

Ironically, if you feel you are holding yourself back when you conform and serve, you are not humble. When you conform to team culture and serve others as part of moving fast and doing God's will, you are humble. You are *contributing*.

> You take people as far as they will go, not as far as you would like them to go.
> **Jeannette Rankin** *(1880 – 1973), American politician and women's rights advocate.*

When I am here (in Milan) I do not fast on Saturday, when in Rome I do fast on Saturday.
Ambrose of Milan (339 – 397), theologian and statesman.

You can have everything in life you want, if you will just help other people get what they want.
Hilary "Zig" Ziglar (1926 – 2012), American author and motivational speaker.

Harmony 2 – mastering ourselves

When we are alone, God is served by *saying what we will do, then doing what we said we would do* (keeping New Year's resolutions, keeping appointments, and completing to-do lists).

An improvement proxy

God does not *directly* care if we complete our to-do lists. At confession, we do not have to mention every time we were five minutes late to a meeting.

However, having the *ability* to say what we will do and always do it *indicates* we have mastered ourselves – we are mature, responsible, God-fearing **adults** – the *true* quality God desires of us.

In other words, saying what we will do and always doing it is an ***improvement proxy*** for being what God wants us to be. An improvement proxy is *a substitute skill which is easier to improve than an original skill, and, when improved, causes the original skill to improve.*

It is hard to quantify if we were more mature on Friday than we were on Thursday.

It is easier to quantify if we did what we said we would do better on Friday than we did on Thursday.

If your personal style is to make a long list in the morning and then do as much as you can on that long list during the day, that is fine. What is important is being able to truthfully say to yourself at the end of the day, "I did what I set out to do today".

> As human beings, our greatness lies not so much in being able to remake the world – that is the myth of the atomic age – as in being able to remake ourselves.
> **Mahatma Gandhi** *(1869-1948), Indian political and spiritual leader.*

> Your visions will become clear only when you can look into your own heart. Who looks outside, dreams; who looks inside, awakes.
> **Carl Gustav Jung** *(1875 – 1961), Swiss psychiatrist and psychoanalyst.*

> I count him braver who overcomes his desires than him who overcomes his enemies.
> **Aristotle** *(384-322 BC), Greek philosopher.*

Take smaller bites

Always doing what you say you will do is not easy, but it is very straightforward. If you are biting off more than you can chew, don't chew harder – instead, take smaller bites.

Do not try to use greater will power to complete self-assignments. Instead, assign yourself fewer and fewer tasks, until you always complete them. Then gradually increase your self-assignments back to any desired level, maintaining compliance.

In other words, use the ***at-the-same-time metric*** of [not struggling AND working hard AND doing what you say you will do] to help guide yourself to self-mastery.

Other proxies

Saying what you will do and always doing it is the most important self-mastery improvement proxy.

Other proxies that indicate self-mastery are:

- *Have what you use and use what you have.*
- *Spend less than you earn.*
- *Like the people you are with and be with the people you like.*

False humility

Humility means not tooting your own horn – not pointing out your own strengths – not putting value on your own actions. This type of humility is good.

Humility does *not* mean bragging about your weaknesses.

Bragging about not being able to do what you said you would do feels like you are being humble, but this is a deceptive feeling. It is *false humility*. It is bragging that you are not an adult.

Evil people who have not mastered themselves are a minor nuisance. Evil people who have mastered themselves are very dangerous to society.

You, a good person, not mastering yourself – not being an adult – means one less effective soldier on God's side, fighting evil adults.

Encouraging others to not be adults – to not master themselves – by making it sound "cool" to not do what you said you would do, is worse. It means *several* fewer effective soldiers on God's side.

> Ye are the light of the world. A city that is set on an hill cannot be hid.
> Neither do men light a candle, and put it under a bushel, but on a candlestick; and it giveth light unto all that are in the house.
> *Mathew 5:14-15 King James Bible*

*Harmony is never fully achieved, but once you are purposely **contributing to others** and have switched from struggling toward self-mastery to **reducing struggle** to achieve self-mastery you are ready for Level 3.*

=== Level 3 === Learning From All ===

Learning from all people

Animal instinct leads us to fear and resent those better than ourselves, look down our noses at those worse than ourselves, and blame others for mistakes – none of which involves improvement.

Good self-improvers ignore animal instinct and learn from everybody, good and bad. This allows them to benefit from the results of billions of ongoing life experiments.

> If I am walking with two other men, each of them will serve as my teacher. I will pick out the good points of the one and imitate them, and the bad points of the other and correct them in myself.
> **Confucius** *(551-479 BC), Chinese philosopher.*

Improving tasks

Good self-improvers impose on themselves an ***improvement tax*** (also known as ***sharpening the saw***). For each task they work on, they spend ninety percent of their time *doing*, and ten percent of their time *improving*. This focuses improvement where it is most beneficial.

Learning from time intervals
Good self-improvers review days, weeks, months, and years.

Once you are learning from all people, improving tasks, and learning from time intervals, you are ready for Level 4.

=== Level 4 === Habit Improvement ===
The better your daily habits are, the better your life will be. Using your ability to always do what you say you will do, consciously reinforce good habits and consciously reduce bad habits (focusing on a single habit at a time).

A better name for this than *learning* or *self-improvement* might be ***self-training***.

Eventually, good habits will become engrained (and bad habits un-engrained), and you will stop having to consciously think about them.

> As it is not one swallow or a fine day that makes a spring, so it is not one day or a short time that makes a man blessed and happy.
> **Aristotle** *(384-322 BC), Greek philosopher.*

> We are what we repeatedly do. Excellence, then, is not an act, but a habit.
> **Will Durant** *(1885 – 1981), American writer, historian, and philosopher.*

Once you are able to train yourself, you are ready for Level 5.

=== Level 5 === Goal-Driven Improvement ===
When you reach Level 5 – congratulations.

Set goals. Work hard ***toward*** them (without struggling ***against*** yourself, others, or the world).

A focus of know-how philosophy

Of the five levels of self-improvement, harmony is probably the least understood. Between the two types of harmony – serving others and self-mastery – self-mastery is probably the least understood.

The art of self-mastery could be a beneficial focus of know-how philosophy in the next decade.

Letting things go their own way

True mastery can be gained
By letting things go their own way.
It can't be gained by interfering.
Be content with what you have;
Rejoice in the way things are.
When you realize there is nothing lacking,
The whole world belongs to you.
***Laozi**, also spelled **Lao Tzu** (circa 6th century BC), legendary Chinese sage and author of the Tao Te Ching.*

S23.8 – Mnemonics

Mnemosyne, Goddess of Memory
(1889, lithography)

Ketterlinus Lithography Company

(Trade card from the "Goddesses of the Greeks and Romans" series (N188), issued in 1889 by W.S. Kimball & Co.)

Spaced repetition and the method of loci

Memory enhancement techniques belong more in the realm of natural philosophy and science than they do in the realm of know-how philosophy, but they are included in S23 because they speed up self-improvement.

From Wikipedia:

> **Spaced repetition** is an evidence-based learning technique that is usually performed with flashcards. Newly introduced and more difficult flashcards are shown more frequently, while older and less difficult flashcards are shown less frequently in order to exploit the psychological spacing effect. The use of spaced repetition has been proven to increase the rate of learning.
>
> https://en.wikipedia.org/wiki/Spaced_repetition
> (05/26/2022)

From Wikipedia:

> The **method of loci** is a strategy for memory enhancement, which uses visualizations of familiar spatial environments in order to enhance the recall of information. The method of loci is also known as the memory journey, memory palace, journey method, memory spaces, or mind palace technique.
>
> https://en.wikipedia.org/wiki/Method_of_loci
> (01/29/2023)

S23.9 – Co-Improvement

The Debate of Socrates and Aspasia
(1800, oil on canvas)

Nicolas-André Monsiau (1754 – 1837), French history painter and draughtsman.

(Aspasia was Socrates' mentor)

Three ways of improving yourself that involve other people are *instruction*, *coaching* and *peer pressure engineering*.

Instruction

Instruction – taking classes, reading books, listening to podcasts, watching videos – means absorbing a one-way flow of information. Instruction is very effective.

Coaching

A life coach, a sports coach, a mentor, or a therapist is an experienced person who helps you improve, using two-way personal interaction. Coaching is very effective.

Peer pressure engineering

If you do not have access to an experienced person, or if you want to move beyond the current state of the art, there is a third method of improving with others – forming small learning teams.

As we changed from apes to humans, we were molded by evolution at the individual level and at the tribal level. Tribal evolution caused us to become intelligent and socially cohesive.

The forces of social cohesion are very strong. To use them for self-improvement, S23 labels these forces *peer pressure*. In English, the term peer pressure has a negative connotation. In S23, the term peer pressure is neutral – you can take advantage of peer pressure and use it to reduce struggle and move yourself forward, or you can succumb to peer pressure and be held back.

S23 calls taking advantage of peer pressure *peer pressure engineering*. The basic approach of peer pressure engineering is to conform to large teams while using small teams to aid self-improvement.

Religious peer pressure

Attend a place of worship weekly to take advantage of *religious peer pressure* to:

- reinforce in you a desire to do the right thing,
- help you minimize struggle *against* the world, and
- support your working hard *with* the world for your own and others' benefit.

Improvement peer pressure

For secular change – for secular self-improvement – use *improvement peer pressure*.

As stated in an earlier chapter, when it comes to human nature, you can metaphorically jump in front of the bus, ride the bus, or drive the bus. You can oppose human nature (in which case you will fail), you can do what comes naturally without thinking, or you can understand and guide human nature (without opposing it) to achieve desired results.

Using improvement peer pressure for self-improvement is driving the bus. It is done in small teams with deliberately crafted team cultures that amplify group learning. You must always conform to team culture, but *the smaller a team is, the more control you have over its team culture*.

Learning team

To best take advantage of improvement peer pressure, form a *learning team* of you and a very small number of your peers. Set up rules that produce a team culture that amplifies learning. Meet regularly to help each other improve, following the rules you set up. Occasionally improve the learning-team rules.

The learning team with the better deliberately crafted improvement-friendly team culture – the better set of rules – wins.

This bears repeating. The learning team with the better set of rules wins.

Learning-team rules

Learning-team rules should be tailored to the individuals on the team to produce the desired improvement-friendly team culture. Here are some possible rules.

It is counter-productive to *punish* failure and bad struggle, and it is counter-productive to *reward* failure and bad struggle. It is always beneficial to reward progress. One rule might be *emotionally reward progress and emotionally ignore failure and bad struggle*.

It is helpful to take notes. Since discussion on a learning team resembles a Socratic dialog, S23 calls learning-team notes Socratic meeting minutes. A second rule might be *record and distribute Socratic meeting minutes*.

A third rule might be to *gently discourage victimhood and hubris*. You cannot improve if you think it is the other person's fault, and you cannot improve if you are already perfect.

Consensus of action is needed on teams, even teams dealing with competing ideas. One way to achieve consensus of action is to let each person make decisions for the team, for some fraction of the time. A fourth rule might be to *rotate leadership*.

In lieu of coaching

If three people who would normally each pay a coach $50 per week form a learning team to coach each other, they will collectively save $150 per week. At first, they will be less effective without the experience of a professional coach. If they gradually improve their peer-coaching skills, however, their learning team will eventually become cost-effective.

Cross pollination

If learning-team members join more than one learning team, learning teams will cross-pollinate.

Alcoholics Anonymous, Toastmasters, Freemasonry, and Asklepieion Therapy

Alcoholics Anonymous, Toastmasters, and Freemasonry are well known organizations that use peer pressure engineering to aid improvement.

Asklepieion Therapy is less well-known. It was an approach used to rehabilitate prisoners in the United States in the 1960's and 1970's that succeeded in the short term but failed to catch on in the long term.

Asklepieion Therapy was a type of group therapy in which participants kept each other "authentic" and "true to themselves" using a form of collective Socratic dialog that highlighted inconsistences in the self-images of the prisoners. This dialog was guided by a set of rules developed by American psychiatrist **Martin G. Groder** (1939 – 2007).

It can be argued that Asklepieion Therapy failed to catch on because of tension with the normal peer pressure that keeps prisoners as they currently are.

Even though it did not catch on, it is the opinion of S23 that the short-term success of Asklepieion Therapy showed that with proper peer pressure engineering, prisoners can be rehabilitated.

A focus of know-how philosophy

Instruction is well understood. Coaching is well understood. The art of creating very small learning teams – teams on which members create and conform to a team culture that supports fast learning and improvement – could be a beneficial focus of know-how philosophy in the next decade.

S23.10 – Agile Agile Programming

Ada King, Countess of Lovelace (Ada Lovelace)
(circa 1840, watercolor)

Alfred Edward Chalon (1780 – 1860), Swiss-born British portraitist.

(Ada Lovelace is considered by many to be the first computer programmer)

The development of *agile programming* software development practices in the mid 1990's influenced the ideas in S23. It could be argued that know-how philosophy is "agile philosophy", and that agile programing is a "know-how philosophy".

This chapter presents observations of agile programming.

A history of agile programming

From the 1940's to the mid 1980's, software was developed using an approach similar to that used for hardware development.

A software project of that era often had a requirements document (the problem to be solved), a functional specification (what the software did), and a design specification (how the software did it). This three-document approach assumed software was developed monolithically – in other words, all at once. The approach worked well for small to medium-sized software projects that did not use graphical user interfaces.

Starting in the mid 1980's, as software projects became larger and started using graphical user interfaces, this previously-successful monolithic approach to software development began to fail more and more often.

In response to increasing failures, between 1985 and 1995 ideas were borrowed from TQM (total quality management – a process improvement approach used in manufacturing) to attempt the systematic improvement of *software development*. Unfortunately, these process improvement ideas did not work when applied to software development. In hindsight, this is because software development is expertise, not a predictable process.

In the mid 1990's, software developers started writing about an approach that eventually was called agile programming. Agile programming is a collection of best practices that implicitly treats software development as expertise. Agile programming does work, and results in the systematic improvement of *software* (instead of software development). In other words, the software that is being developed gradually and steadily improves.

In the 2000's the electric car company Tesla and the space company Space X started using an approach similar to agile programming to systematically improve factories, cars, and rockets.

The irony of agile programming

As American philosopher of science **Thomas Kuhn** (1922 – 1996) explains in his book *The Structure of Scientific Revolutions*, when paradigm shifts occur, net benefit occurs, but there is also some loss. When horses and buggies converted to automobiles, drivers lost the ability to fall asleep at the reins.

When software developers gave up failed process-improvement attempts in favor of agile programming, the focus on the improvement of software development was lost.

Today, agile techniques are currently used to improve software, factories, cars, and rockets, but not to systematically improve *software development*.

The irony of agile programming is that it does not improve itself.

Agile agile programming

If two new practices are added to the set of generally accepted agile programming practices (GAAPP), agile programming *will* steadily improve itself.

1) Per-project (not per-company) practices

As with any skill, if you follow all the best practices all the time, you will not innovate and will not improve. If a company has company-wide agile practices that are used for all software projects, little innovation will take place. If a company uses a different set of agile practices for each project, and records what works, then steady long-term software development improvement will occur.

Additionally, in the short-term, since each project is different, a custom-designed set of agile practices will serve a project better than a one-size-fits-all set of practices.

2) Two backlogs

An agile project should use two backlogs. A primary backlog prioritized by the customer controls *feature* development. A secondary backlog of housekeeping tasks prioritized by the software team lead controls improvements to the development *environment*.

This ensures that both feature improvements and environment improvements are accomplished in an efficient order and at an efficient pace.

Also, if housekeeping tasks are worked on ten or twenty percent of the time, in emergencies this time can be reallocated to feature development. This capability acts as a tactical "time reserve" that can help keep a project on schedule.

In summary

Agile agile programming with per-project practices and two backlogs will steadily improve the *software* being developed, the software development *environment*, and *software development* itself.

S23.11 – Synergy

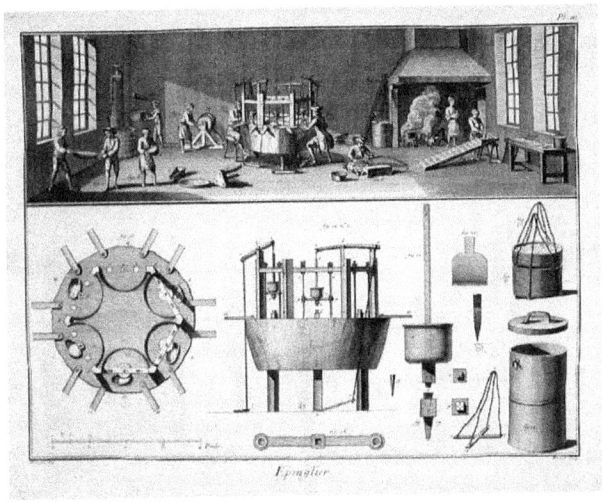

Epinglier, Plate III (Pin Making)
(1762, engraving)

An illustration in *Encyclopédie,* edited by
Denis Diderot *(1713-1784), French philosopher.*

(artist) **Louis-Jacques Goussier** *(1722-1799), French illustrator.*
(engraver) **Benoit Louis Prevost** *(1735-1804), French engraver.*

A single workman (with no machines) can produce at the utmost twenty pins in a day. Ten persons (in a pin factory) can produce upwards of forty-eight thousand pins in a day.

(paraphrased) **Adam Smith** *(1723 – 1790), Scottish economist and philosopher.*

The concept of *synergy* is important for understanding evolution, economics, and society.

In some natural systems and some human systems, the worth of the whole is greater than the sum of the worth of the parts.

1. In a strict sense, the *extra worth* is called synergy, as in *synergy is created*.

2. In a looser sense,

    a. the *event* of two or more items combining to create worth is called synergy, as in *synergy occurs*, or
    b. two or more items that create synergy when they join are said to *have synergy*, or
    c. a field or area of study within which synergy occurs is also said to *have synergy*.

Evolutionary synergy means that the fitness of a team can be greater than the sum of the fitness of the individuals composing the team. In other words, belonging to a smoothly working team can result in more surviving progeny for an organism. This drives evolution to produce ever better teams.

Teams of humans have ***economic synergy***. In Adam Smith's pin factory example, the output of ten pin makers is much greater when they work together than when they work separately. When people form a company, the company has more worth than the sum of the worth of the individuals forming the company. In other words, forming a company creates worth.

Teams of humans have ***military synergy***. A coordinated army of 1,000 soldiers will defeat 1,000 individuals. Better synergy (a better-coordinated army) will defeat worse synergy (a worse-coordinated army of the same size).

Three types of *social glue* hold societies together, enabling economic synergy and military synergy: ***religion, culture***, and ***politics***.

There is a fourth type of synergy that is not discussed in S23, but implied. That is the academic synergy that occurs when religion, science, and philosophy are defined and pursued in such a way that they complement each other, rather than conflict with each other.

Religion, science, and philosophy can be thought of as three horses working together to pull humanity forward in a Russian troika (racing to stay ahead of the four horsemen of the apocalypse).

S23.12 – The Evolution of Evolution

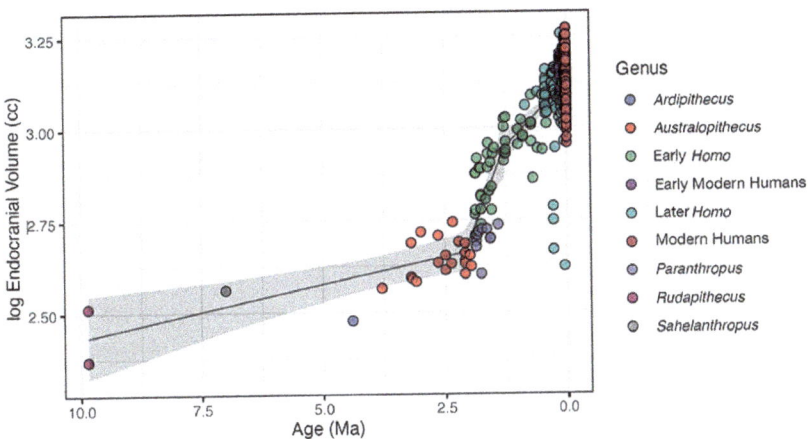

Chart copied from Wikipedia showing evolution of brain size from apes to modern humans. The rate of change of brain size increased dramatically about two million years ago. This increase in rate-of-change implies an increase in evolutionary pressure.

https://en.wikipedia.org/wiki/Brain_size (3/13/2023)

By Authors of the study: Brian Villmoare and Mark Grabowski - https://www.frontiersin.org/articles/10.3389/fevo.2022.963568/full, CC BY 4.0, https://commons.wikimedia.org/w/index.php?curid=122405325

To understand human improvement, it helps to understand how human brains work. To understand how human brains work, it helps to understand how human brains evolved. Hence this chapter.

When God created the Earth about four and a half billion years ago, He imbued it with physical laws, economic principles, and evolutionary principles.

The best-known evolutionary principle is *survival of the fittest*.

However, evolution is also driven by a second principle – the principle of *team fitness*. Because of synergy, the fitness of a team can be greater than the sum of the fitness of individual team members, meaning there is fitness in belonging to a team. This principle causes ever-more complex life forms to emerge and dominate. It is almost a foil or counter to physical entropy.

The team fitness principle caused archaea and bacteria to combine into single cell eukaryotes, and eukaryotes to combine into multi-cellular animals, fungi, and plants. It caused packs and herds to emerge, and it caused hominids to combine into ever-larger social groups.

As organisms became more complex, evolution became more complex, more powerful, and faster working, in a positive feedback loop.

Science will eventually have the final say. But where science has yet to tread, philosophy must make guesses. When trying to understand evolution, guesses are still needed to answer several big evolutionary questions.

Question 1 – Which came first – sexual reproduction or multicellular life?
In other words, how did multi-cellular life evolve?

S23 assumes sexual reproduction came first. S23 believes single cell eukaryotes invented sexual reproduction – a way to randomly combine DNA from two parent cells into the DNA of a single child cell, so that each child cell had a different combination of DNA. This new gene-shuffling capability greatly increased the speed and power of evolution. This faster and more powerful evolution then created multicellular animals, fungi, and plants.

Question 2 – HOW did instinct evolve?

Why brains and instinct evolved is easy to answer – multi-cellular animals needed a way to control themselves. When there is a need, evolution provides a solution.

How brains and instinct evolved is harder to answer. The fact that instinct is encoded in DNA is obvious. Baby animals that hatch from eggs and have no contact with their parents instinctively do many complicated things – they hunt for food, avoid enemies, and are attracted to mates.

Perhaps the right question to ask is *where and how is the wiring of the brain encoded in DNA?* To answer this question, S23 makes five guesses.

1) The DNA that encodes for *genes* and the DNA that encodes for *gene-switches* take up a small percentage of total DNA. S23 guesses that *brain-wiring* instructions are encoded in the remaining regions of DNA – the regions that are traditionally called junk DNA or non-coding DNA.

2) S23 guesses that the *mechanism* of brain-wiring encoding in DNA is different than the mechanism of gene encoding, and different than the mechanism of gene-switch encoding.

3) S23 guesses that these three different encoding mechanisms evolve at three different rates.

4) S23 guesses that the mechanism of brain-wiring encoding took two hundred million years to evolve, starting seven hundred million years ago when multicellular animals first emerged. At the end of those two hundred million years, when evolution had mastered the art of brain-wiring encoding in DNA, instinct began to steadily evolve.

5) When instinct began to steadily evolve, animal behavior began to steadily evolve. Soon after animal behavior began to steadily evolve, predators evolved – animals that hunted other animals. S23 believes that predation set up an evolutionary arms race between predators and their prey, which caused the Cambrian explosion about five hundred million years ago.

Rewording the first three ideas above results in the following philosophical model of DNA, comprising three mechanisms:

1) Mechanism X encodes for genes and evolves slowly. This type of DNA controls an animal's chemistry and takes up a small fraction of total DNA.

2) Mechanism Y encodes for gene switches and evolves at a medium pace. Although this type of DNA is used throughout life, it is especially used during embryonic development. It controls an organism's size and shape – an organism's structure – and also takes up a small fraction of total DNA.

3) Mechanism Z encodes for brain-wiring and evolves at a fast pace. This type of DNA controls an animal's

behavior and takes up a large fraction of total DNA (which is traditionally called junk DNA or non-controlling DNA).

Mechanisms X and Y are known. Scientists understand how genes are encoded in DNA and are steadily learning how gene switches are encoded in DNA.

The existence of mechanism Z is an opinion. S23 does not even guess how mechanism Z works, but perhaps the computer science technique of "genetic algorithms" holds a clue.

Two reasons gene-switch evolution and brain-wiring evolution occur faster than gene evolution are:

1) Gene switch encoding and brain-wiring encoding are *additive*. If a gene switch that codes for tall combines with a gene switch that codes for short the result will be a gene switch that codes for average. Likewise, if an instinct to run combines with an instinct to fight, the result will be an instinct to remain in a defensive position.

2) Gene-switch encoding and brain-wiring encoding are more *tolerant of mutations* than gene encoding is. A slightly different body shape or slightly different behavior has less chance of catastrophic failure than a slightly different chemistry.

Question 3 – WHY did human intelligence evolve?

For five hundred million years, animals controlled themselves by instinct. Suddenly, starting two million years ago, one genus, and one genus only, quickly became intelligent. *How* our ancestors became intelligent is answered above – brains can evolve fast for any needed purpose. But *why* did intelligence suddenly become needed?

S23 guesses that intra-species *no-retreat warfare*, around a lake shore, caused our ancestors to suddenly start needing intelligence a little over two million years ago.

The opinion of no-retreat-warfare evolution

An opinion is to philosophy as a theory is to science. Here is S23's opinion of intra-species no-retreat-warfare evolution.

Tied to the lake shore

Our ancestors evolved hands while living in the trees of the African jungle. Five to seven million years ago, as the climate of east Africa changed, our ancestors came down from the trees onto the savanna and evolved into Genus Ardipithecus and then Genus Australopithecus.

At some point, probably three to four million years ago, a group of Australopithecines migrated to the shore of one of Africa's great lakes in the rift valley and began using their hands and rudimentary stone tools to catch and eat fish and shellfish. Still driven by instinct, they became dependent on this lake-shore diet. For S23, we invent a name for this group - Australopithecus [lake shore]. This made-up name represents whatever real species was tied to the lake shore by diet.

The idea of some of our evolution taking place at the water's edge is not new. In 1960, English marine biologist **Alister Hardy** (1896 - 1985) proposed an "Aquatic Ape Hypothesis".

From Wikipedia:

> The **aquatic ape hypothesis** ... postulates that the ancestors of modern humans took a divergent evolutionary pathway from the other great apes by becoming adapted to a more aquatic habitat.

https://en.wikipedia.org/wiki/Aquatic_ape_hypothesis
(4/28/2022)

Many mammals are semi-aquatic, such as hippopotamuses, manatees, polar bears, otters, and beavers. According to Hardy and other proponents, our upright posture, nose shape, hairlessness, subcutaneous fat, and webbed fingers were affected by our ancestors adopting a semi-aquatic lifestyle for some length of time.

Accidental Deaths

Occasional squabbles between troops of A. [lake shore] resulted in death (possibly by drowning, possibly by being hit on the head with the stone tools used to open shellfish, and possibly by both).

In nature, a losing animal, or group of animals, retreats. And at first, losing A. [lake shore] troops did retreat. But at some point, because they were tied to a circular one-dimensional lake shore, they could retreat no further.

Evolution is affected

At this point, accidental deaths started affecting evolution. Those who killed had more surviving offspring than those who were killed. And as soon as killing started affecting evolution, evolution started affecting killing.

This bears repeating. As soon as intra-species killing started affecting evolution, evolution started affecting intra-species killing.

And not just any evolution. Intra-species no-retreat-warfare evolution was more powerful and worked faster than any type of evolution that had come before it in the four-billion-year history of Earth. The amount of change that evolution accomplished in the past two million years (between apes and man) may be as great as the amount of change that evolution accomplished in the previous sixty million years (between mammals of the dinosaur age and apes).

What did this powerful and fast-working evolution give us? Larger bodies? Stronger muscles? Surprisingly, no. Mostly, no-retreat warfare caused us to relentlessly evolve better intelligence and (ironically) better social cohesiveness. Small troops of instinct-driven Genus Australopithecus evolved into large tribes of thought-guided Genus Homo.

A three-fold problem

What can the opinion of no-retreat-warfare evolution tell us about our modern selves? To answer this question, we must first understand how no-retreat-warfare evolution worked.

To work, no-retreat-warfare evolution had to be self-sustaining. And to be self-sustaining, no-retreat-warfare evolution had to solve a three-fold problem.

First, how could the exact same species, with the exact same DNA, contain an "us" and a "them"? Second, once an "us" and a "them" were identified, how could the same species be compelled to be nice to an "us" and mean to a "them"? Third, once the current "us" or the current "them" won – once there was no longer an external enemy – how could the winning cohesive society quickly split into two new antagonists – a new "us" and a new "them"?

God, language, and culture

The solution that no-retreat-warfare evolution came up with to this near impossible three-fold problem is fascinating. S23 believes that multiple brain receptacles evolved. One brain receptacle evolved for religion (sometimes called the conscience or super-ego), one brain receptacle evolved for language and grammar, and one brain receptacle evolved for culture.

These receptacles are different than hard-wired instinct, and different than the areas of the brain designed to store knowledge and skill. They contain rules. Rules are harder to insert into the brain then knowledge or skill, and once stored they are harder to change or remove. When rules are violated, they produce the emotion of "shame".

The *wiring* of brain receptacles is encoded in our DNA. The *content* of brain receptacles (a set of rules) is not encoded in DNA. Rather, it is added throughout life (mostly in childhood). In the best case it is added by parents and ministers. In the worst case it is added by gang leaders and anarchists.

The concept of brain receptacles is not new. American linguist and philosopher **Noam Chomsky** (1928 -) postulated a theory of "universal grammar" which included the concept of a language acquisition device.

From Wikipedia:

> The **Language Acquisition Device** (LAD) is a claim from language acquisition research proposed by Noam Chomsky in the 1960s. The LAD concept is a purported instinctive mental capacity which enables an infant to acquire and produce language.
>
> https://en. /wiki/Language_acquisition_device
> (4/29/2022)

There is no biological reason that morality, language, and culture could not be hard-wired into the brain. But if this happened, intra-species no-retreat-warfare evolution would stop working. A winning tribe would not split into two groups – a new "us" and a new "them". They would continue to live peacefully. And eventually they would be conquered by a tribe that did not stop evolving.

Similar to hectosophies

It is interesting to note that no-retreat-warfare evolution (which caused an explosive growth in our intelligence and social cohesion) and hectosophies (which caused an explosive growth in S23's ideas – hopefully some of them useful) work using the same mechanism. It is not even an analogous mechanism – it is the very same mechanism – a growing population competing in a fixed-size arena.

Warfare-based evolution (post-lake)

We needed a no-retreat arena to jumpstart warfare-based evolution and cause it to become self-sustaining. Once it became self-sustaining, however, warfare-based evolution continued as Genus Homo roamed the Earth. It occurred faster whenever and wherever tribes could not retreat, but it also occurred (albeit at a slower rate) when and where tribes could retreat.

It is interesting to note that from two million years ago to ten thousand years ago, technology (stone, bone, and wood tools) evolved very slowly. S23 believes that during this time tool improvement took a back seat to intelligence improvement and culture improvement.

Warfare-based evolution (from agriculture)

About ten thousand years ago, when our ancestors discovered agriculture, this dynamic changed. Agriculture again tied us to one location. Evolution again sped up. However, this evolution was different.

Agriculture required technology. Better technology meant better agriculture. Better agriculture meant more tribe members. More tribe members won more wars. Thus, better technology won wars, and so it started affecting evolution.

And as soon as technology started affecting evolution, evolution started affecting technology.

This bears repeating. As soon as technology started affecting evolution, evolution started affecting technology.

Non-genetic evolution

This time, however, the evolution was external to our bodies. It was not DNA evolution. It was technology evolution.

Technology evolves each time two or three previous inventions are combined into a new invention, or each time existing technology is put to a new use. It is true evolution – new technology builds on top of old technology the same way new lifeforms build on top of old lifeforms.

River valleys

Technology evolution started in the agriculture-enabled no-retreat arenas of the Euphrates and Tigris Rivers in Mesopotamia, the Nile River in Egypt, the Yellow River in China, and the Indus River in India.

In the Western Hemisphere technology advanced around Lake Texcoco in Mexico and along the narrow coast and adjoining mountains of Peru.

Once the genie was out of the bottle – once Pandora's box was opened – once technology evolution started – there was no stopping it.

Should we continue to fight each other?

No. Just because we evolved our backbones in the ocean does not mean we should return to the ocean. Just because we evolved our hands by living in trees does not mean we should return to living in trees. And just because we evolved our intelligence by no-retreat warfare does not mean we should return to continuous no-retreat warfare.

Should we pretend our intelligence did not come from warfare?

No. Full knowledge of ourselves (for example why we so readily divide into two competing camps in the absence of an external enemy, why we need to teach morality to our children, and why we need to be patriotic yet tolerant – to believe our own system of government and religion is best while still fully respecting others' governments and religions) is crucial to maintaining peace.

Reminder: this is not science

This chapter needs a reminder that this is a philosophy book, and not a science or history book.

Each idea in S23 is a subjective opinion, and nothing in S23 pretends to be a scientific hypothesis, scientific theory, or historical fact. Science and history depend on *evidence* because they are based on *consensus*. No evidence is presented in S23 and no consensus is expected.

Charting the evolution of evolution

The following chart shows the evolution of lifeforms and the evolution of evolution. Again, nothing in S23 is science – the chart is the opinion of S23.

Lifeform	Evolutionary Mechanism	Evolutionary Pressure	Duration (years)
replicating soup	random mutation	only the environment	1.5 B
prokaryotes	fission with mutation of genes	bacterial predation (arms race 1)	
eukaryotes	single-cell mating	single cell predation (arms race 2)	1.5 B
multicellular animals, fungi, and plants	multicellular organisms with mating [three types of DNA encoding – genes (for chemistry), gene switches (for size and shape), and brain wiring (for instinct)]	animals eating eukaryotes (arms race 3) animals eating plants (arms race 4)	200 M instinct gradually forms
		animals eating animals (arms race 5)	500 M instinct now
animal herds and packs		herd grazing and pack predation (arms race 6)	works and starts evolving
genus Homo	brain "receptacles" for religion, language, and culture	intra-species no-retreat warfare (tied to a lake shore)	2 M instinct replaced by thought
Homo Sapiens	older technology begets newer technology	no-retreat warfare (from agriculture)	10 K writing aids thought

S23.13 – Team Worth

An Economic Hectosophy

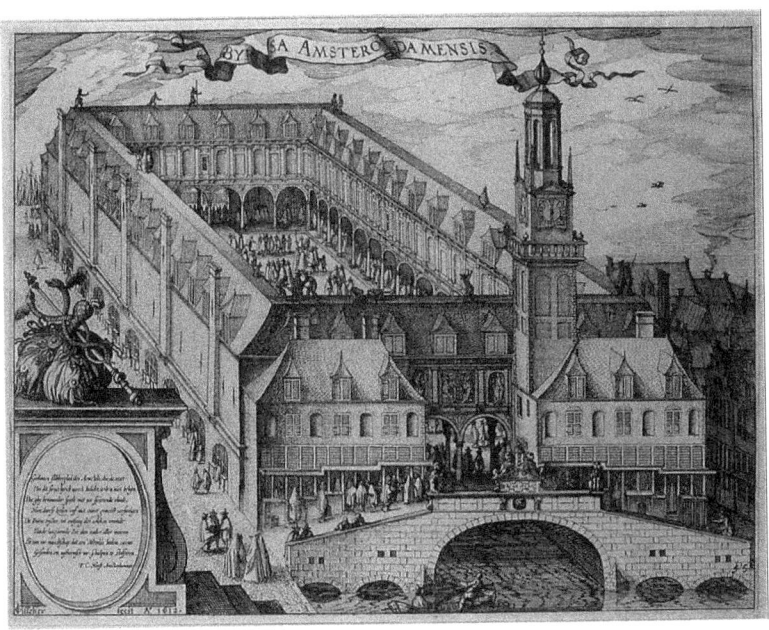

Amsterdam Stock Exchange
(1612, engraving)

Claes Janszoon Visscher (1587 – 1652), Dutch engraver, mapmaker, and publisher.

(Amsterdam's Hendrick de Keyser Stock Exchange, built in 1611, is often considered to be the first modern stock exchange)

Economic opinions

This chapter presents personal economic opinions, collected and expanded over a period of several years.

A riddle

Gary and Maria have $100,000 in the bank. They decide to build a house. They pay $100,000 to an architect, contractor, and workers to construct the house. They end up with a $100,000 house, and, after expenses, the architect, contractor, and workers end up with $50,000 in the bank. Where did the extra $50,000 come from?

Another riddle

Peggy, Kerry, Celia, and Liz start a company. Investors have $1 million to invest. The investors buy half the new company's stock for $1 million, and the founders keep the other half of the stock. The business has $1 million in the bank, and no other assets, but is valued at $2 million. Where does the extra $1 million of worth come from?

The worth of work hours and business hours

The $50,000 of new worth in Gary and Peggy's house seems to have been extracted from the work hours put in by the architect, contractor, and workers.

The $1 million of worth created by the four entrepreneurs seems to represent the worth of future profits of the business. Since profits come from the operation of the company, the extra $1 million can be said to represent the worth of future business hours.

A definition of worth

It seems that hours of work, or hours of a business's operation, have worth. It is accepted that current hours of work have worth – workers are paid for hours of work delivered. But future hours of work also have worth – when you make a purchase using a credit card, you are paying with future hours of work, which can also be described as future earnings. You can buy, sell, and trade future earnings today.

Thus, we make the following definitions of worth:

1. An individual's total worth is equal to the sum of the worth of the individual's tangible assets and the worth of the individual's future earnings.

2. A business's total worth is equal to the sum of the worth of its tangible assets and the worth of its future earnings.

We expand on businesses in a later section; for this section we concentrate on individuals.

Applying the first definition, a college graduate, with no tangible assets, is worth what her anticipated future income stream is worth today. The worth of a future income stream can be said to be the amount of money in the bank that would generate the same stream of income. If the college graduate expects to make $25,000 a year for the rest of her life, her current worth is the amount of money that can generate $25,000 a year, or around $250,000 (assuming, for simplicity, that money earns 10% interest).

A retired person, with $250,000 in the bank and no anticipated future income, is thus also worth $250,000.

Good news. By adopting this philosophy, the college graduate, who by most common definitions has zero monetary worth, suddenly has $250,000 of monetary worth.

Bad news. This worth takes into account all the graduate's future earnings, so it somehow applies a figure of worth to the rest of her life. If nothing else changes, the graduate would go through life always worth about $250,000, slowly consuming some earnings and converting other earnings into tangible assets. If the graduate borrowed heavily and spent all that worth in one year, she would have no money left for the rest of her life.

More good news. Though this definition of worth covers a whole lifetime, *this worth can be changed*. Anything that alters the worth of the college graduate's future earnings or tangible assets (up or down) will alter her current worth.

Increasing the worth of future earnings

What happens if the college graduate goes to graduate school? Let's say graduate school costs $50,000 and increases her anticipated future income to $50,000 per year. She is now worth $500,000. She has gained $250,000 of worth for the price of $50,000, a net gain of $200,000.

Can this increase in worth be spent? Yes. When she commits to going to graduate school, the student can take out a school loan, and spend some of this new future worth to attend graduate school.

From where does this increase in worth come? With a little reflection, the gain in worth comes from an increase in the *value of the graduate's time*.

A scientist is taught that physical things obey a "law of conservation" – matter cannot be created or destroyed, only altered. New matter must come from some transformation of old matter, with no loss.

However, the *value* of the graduate's time is not a physical thing; it is a "market" thing. It has no mass or momentum. It does not obey physical laws. It obeys "market" laws. And it is not against market laws for value to change.

Although we present no proof, we assert that an increase in the value of a person's time (and in their worth) does not subtract from someone else's worth. The worth is *created*. It is not transferred.

In summary:

3. An individual's worth can be increased by increasing the value of the individual's time, thus increasing the worth of future earnings. This increase in worth does not subtract from someone else's worth. It is created.

How can the value of an individual's time be increased?

Three ways of increasing the value of an individual's time (in other words, an individual's productivity) come to mind.

A) An individual can acquire a better tool, which makes him more productive. (A carpenter who discards a hand saw and buys a power saw increases the value of his future earnings).

B) An individual can adopt a better process, or learn something new, which makes him more productive. (A plumber who discovers that cutting pipe on site will save him 10% of his time increases the value of his future earnings).

C) An individual can team up with other individuals, making all the individuals more productive. (A person good at hunting and a person good at gathering vegetables will be more productive working together than working separately).

Three ways of gaining productivity from teams come to mind.

a) If two (or more) individuals have mismatched skills, they can specialize. A good hunter can hunt all day and a good vegetable gatherer can gather all day.

b) Two (or more) individuals can gain from economies of scale. Even if their skills are the same, one person can shop for two people, and one person can cook for two people, and each will gain productivity.

c) Two (or more) individuals can gain from reinforcement. Because humans are social, working side by side often makes people more productive.

Summarizing:

4. The value of an individual's time, and therefore the individual's worth, can be increased by the individual
    joining a team with mismatched skills,
    joining a team with economies of scale,
    joining a team with reinforcement,
    acquiring better tools, or
    acquiring better knowledge and processes.

Who gets to keep the extra worth?

When one person increases her worth by buying a tool or going to school, she gets to keep all of the gain. When a group of people increase their worth by forming a team, who gets to keep the gain?

We struggled with this question, and did not discover an answer until reading a New York Times article about William Vickrey, the late Nobel laureate economist from Columbia. The article talked about Vickrey's theories of efficient auctions, where the winner of a closed-bid auction should pay what the second highest bidder bids.

The answer to who gets to keep the extra worth generated by a team is fascinating:

5. *The owner or organizer of a team gets to keep all the leftover team worth, after paying other team members for being on the team. Theoretically, in a seller's market (fewer workers than jobs), the owner must pay each team member $1 more than the second richest rival team can afford to pay. In a buyer's market (more workers than jobs), the owner can hire each team member for $1 less than the second cheapest rival team member can afford to participate for.*

Several examples are in order.

A doctor earns $50 per hour. A housecleaner has expenses of $5 per hour. The doctor hires the housecleaner for one hour per week, at $10 per hour, making a temporary team of two. Assuming the doctor gets to work one more hour, $45 of worth is being created each week by the team. The doctor is keeping $40 of the extra worth; the housecleaner $5.

There are three doctors, earning respectively $80, $60, and $50 per hour. There is only one housecleaner available for one hour, with expenses of $5 per hour. The $80 doctor will hire the housecleaner for $60, and the other doctors will do their own housecleaning. $75 of worth is being created, the doctor is keeping $20, and the housecleaner is keeping $55.

There is one doctor, earning $50 per hour. There are three housecleaners, with expenses respectively of $9, $7, and $5 per hour. The doctor will hire the $5 housecleaner for $7 per hour. $45 of worth is being created, the doctor is keeping $43, and the housecleaner is keeping $2.

An owner-manager forms a business by hiring five other workers. The business makes a profit of $200 per hour, after non-labor expenses. Because of market forces, the owner-manager must pay the workers $30, $30, $20, $10, and $10 per hour. The owner-manager gets to keep the remaining $100 per hour.

A non-working owner forms a similar business by hiring a manager and five workers. The business also makes a profit of $200 per hour, after non-labor expenses. Because of market forces, the owner must pay the manager $70 per hour, and must pay the workers the same $30, $30, $20, $10, and $10 per hour. The owner gets to keep the remaining $30 per hour.

It is interesting to note that an efficient business can afford to pay an employee more than a less-efficient business can. This is because:

6. *The same employee generates more worth for an efficient business than for a less-efficient business.*

Increasing the worth of tangible assets

Since the worth of an individual is equal to the sum of the worth of tangible assets and the worth of future earnings, an individual's worth can also be increased by increasing the worth of his tangible assets. This can be done by exchanging some of his assets for other assets that are worth more.

By exchanging assets we mean buying and selling, or trading. In voluntary trades (as opposed to some form of theft), both sides gain worth, else the trade would not take place.

How do both sides gain?

Assume there are two parties in a trade. Again using the argument that value does not obey the laws of physics, an item can be worth a different amount to each of the two parties. By moving from one party to another, the value of an item increases; therefore worth is created. Both sides share this worth.

One example of trade is barter. A hunter gives a farmer a rabbit in return for a basket of turnips. To the hunter, the rabbit is worth one hour of time; the basket of turnips two hours of time. To the farmer, the basket of turnips is worth one hour of time; the rabbit two hours of time. The trade creates one hunter-hour plus one farmer-hour of worth, with each party sharing part of the created worth.

Money is a neutral facilitator of bartering that allows one half of a barter to take place independently of the other half. Using the concept of money, the example can be restated as a sale. A hunter has a rabbit that is worth $10 to him and worth $20 to a farmer. The hunter sells the rabbit to the farmer for $15. Both the hunter and the farmer gain $5 of worth.

How is the gain divided?

Market forces determine how a gain in worth from trade is divided. Market forces can best be illustrated by further examples.

There are three hunters, each with a similar rabbit, and one farmer, who wants a rabbit. To the farmer, a rabbit is worth $20. To the hunters, their rabbits are worth $10, $12, and $15 respectively. The farmer buys a rabbit from the first hunter for $12. $10 of worth is created; the hunter gets $2 of the gain, and the farmer gets $8 of the gain.

There is one hunter with a rabbit worth $10 to him. There are three farmers, each of whom wants the rabbit. The rabbit is worth $15, $18, and $20 respectively to the farmers. The hunter sells the third farmer the rabbit for $18. $10 of worth is created; the hunter gets $8 of the gain, the farmer gets $2 of the gain.

Summarizing:

7. Both parties gain worth in a voluntary sale or trade, because items change value when they change ownership. The distribution of the gain in worth is determined by market forces.

What assets have value?

Assets that meet needs have value (food, shelter, clothing). Assets that are tools that increase the value of an individual's time, or save an individual time, have value (powered lawn mowers, cars, college educations). Belonging to teams has an important effect on the value of an individual's time, so assets that improve team cohesion have value (sporting events, club memberships, social skills).

Since owning or organizing a team has the largest effect on the value of an individual's time, assets that facilitate leadership have great value. Management training comes to mind; however, the assets that have the largest affect on an individual's leadership position are *status symbols*.

People, among their many instincts, have both the instinct to lead teams, and the instinct to follow team leaders. Both these instincts somehow recognize status symbols. The earliest descriptions of tribal leaders note the trinkets and doodads the leaders possessed. Today, the better-dressed person, or the person with the nicer car, gets more respect.

What makes a status symbol

Rarity. No matter how much value an item adds to a person's time, if everybody has it, it cannot denote position. The rarer an item is, the fewer people there are that can posses a copy, and the higher an individual's position must be for that individual to posses a copy. If only one purple robe exists, only the highest-ranking person will have one. The robe will then identify that person's position to the instincts of her followers.

Showing a status symbol is the slightly more civilized equivalent of flexing your muscles or baring your teeth, to demonstrate economic power.

To summarize:

8. *Assets that provide for needs, multiply the worth of time, or denote leadership position have worth, in roughly that order. Assets have different worth for different people.*

Businesses
We restate our previous definition: a business's worth is equal to the sum of the worth of its tangible assets and the worth of its future earnings.

Stock
Since a share of stock represents a fraction of the ownership of a business, the same assertion holds for a single share of stock: the worth of a share of stock is equal to the sum of the worth of the assets per share, and the worth of future earnings per share. A business with $10 worth of assets per share, which earns an unchanging $2 per year per share, is worth ($10 + $20) per share, or $30 per share (assuming $2 per year is worth $20, which is the amount of money in the bank at 10% interest needed to generate the $2 per year).

Growing and shrinking
A business with no assets that earns $2 per year per share, and whose earnings increase at a constant 5% per year, is theoretically worth the amount of money in a bank that can generate the same growing income stream, or $40 per share (assuming the money in the bank gets 10% interest).

Likewise, business with no assets earning $2 per year per share with earnings decreasing at a constant 5% per year is worth $13.33 per share.

The business with no assets earning $2 per year per share, whose earnings increase at a constant 15% per year, is theoretically worth an infinite amount, because no amount of money in the bank at 10% interest can generate a yearly stream of earnings that grows that fast.

There are practical limits on size and lifespan, however – a business that grows too large becomes inefficient and a business that exists too long becomes sclerotic.

Growth is important

Company assets	Earnings per share	Growth per year	Worth per share*
$0	$2	0	$20
$0	$2	5%	$40
$0	$2	-5%	$13.33

* assumes an interest rate of 10% (for lower interest rates, growth is more important)

Worth, value, and price

Since the theoretical worth of a share of stock is unknown in real life, each owner places her own value on a share of stock.

These owner values differ, for three main reasons. First, although the law ensures all owners have access to information needed to make good estimates, this access costs time (and therefore money), and so is self-rationed by each owner. Second, even with the same access to information, experienced owners make better estimates than inexperienced owners. Third, similar owners pursuing different investment strategies will place different values on the same share of stock.

Thus, three concepts exist for each share of stock – the (unknown) theoretical worth of the share, the value each owner places on the share, and the price of the share, determined by market forces acting on the set of owner values.

To note

It is interesting to note that as bank interest rates drop to zero, using our definition of worth, all individuals and companies approach an infinite worth. At this time, we do not fully understand the implications of this observation, or what the countering forces are.

It is also interesting to note that instead of using a theoretical amount of money in the bank to assign a value to an income stream ($2 per year = $20 in the bank), we can use a theoretical amount of money invested in the stock market ($2 per year = $? in the stock market). We do not understand the implications of this, either.

Formulas used

The worth of a constant stream of future earnings is equal to the amount of money in a bank which, multiplied by the interest rate, will produce the same earnings stream.

$$m \times i = e$$
$$m = e/i$$

where

e = yearly earnings
i = yearly interest rate
m = money in bank for yearly earnings

The worth of a *growing* stream of future earnings is equal to the sum of two amounts of money in a bank. One amount multiplied by the interest rate will produce the non-growing earnings stream. The other amount multiplied by the interest rate will increase both amounts of money in the bank by the growth rate.

$$m_e \times i = e$$
$$m_e = e/i$$

$$m_g \times i = (m_e + m_g) \times g$$
$$(m_g \times i) - (m_g \times g) = m_e \times g$$
$$m_g \times (i - g) = m_e \times g$$
$$m_g = m_e \times g/(i - g)$$

$$m = m_e + m_g$$
$$m = m_e + (m_e \times g/(i - g))$$
$$m = m_e \times (1 + g/(i - g))$$
$$\boxed{m = e/i \times (1 + g/(i - g))}$$

where

e = yearly earnings
g = growth rate of yearly earnings (where $g < i$)
i = yearly interest rate
m_e = money in bank for non-growing yearly earnings
m_g = money in bank for growth of money in bank
m = total money in bank for growing yearly earnings

Starting and growing a business

One way to start a business is as follows. A single organizer, or group of organizers, forms a team. This team has worth today – the worth of its future earnings. The organizers sell some of this worth in the form of stock. The organizers use the proceeds of the sale to operate the business until the business earns enough to cover day-to-day operations.

In another case, a business decides to grow. This planned growth has worth today – the worth of the extra future earnings. The business uses some of this worth by taking out a loan to fund the growth.

Owners benefit most

Because the owner or organizer of a team gets to keep excess team worth, and because it usually (though not always) takes money to form a new business team, the already rich are usually the ones who end up owning, and therefore benefiting the most, from new businesses. Thus, as the cliché states, the rich get richer.

Actually, since for one person to acquire more worth (without using force), everybody he deals with must also gain worth, a more accurate cliché would be:

The rich get richer faster.

Landowners and capitalists

Before the 1800's, rich people owned land, and landowners became rich. During the 1800's and 1900's, rich people owned factories, and factory owners (capitalists) became rich.

In the past, land and capital seemed economically special. This is understandable, but they were not special. Their visibility obscured the underlying reality, which was that owning a team – being the one who got to keep profit – was what was economically special.

Inheritance taxes

Most countries impose high inheritance taxes. Like a firebreak, inheritance taxes diminish the rich-get-richer-faster spiral as it tries to move from generation to generation.

Positive and negative competition

The drive to become rich seems to be fueled by the instincts to beat competitors and to lead teams. These instincts are strong and manifest themselves in two forms: moving ahead faster than competitors (positive competition), or holding competitors back (negative competition).

Since creating worth is not a zero-sum game, these two manifestations do not produce the same result. If an individual or business, and their competitors, are creating worth as fast as they can, and one pulls ahead, this is good for the economy as a whole. Worth is being created at a maximum rate. If an individual or business is somehow preventing their competitors from creating worth as fast as they can, some potential worth is not being created. The economy grows slower than it could.

Holding others back may or may not be intentional. One example of holding others back is that if some resource useful for acquiring worth is limited, the first group to become rich can monopolize that resource. In effect, they shut the door behind themselves, intentionally or not. Up until the nineteenth century, land was often the limiting resource for creating worth, and ownership of land often divided the rich from the not rich.

Self regulation

Honest businesses want to do no harm (e.g., pollute, exploit workers, or produce dangerous products). If doing no harm adds cost, businesses self-regulate, or help the government write regulations, to prevent dishonest companies gaining an unfair cost advantage by doing harm. Self regulation by honest companies is good.

Greed, profit, and shareholder value

Greedy companies chase profit and short-term shareholder value. A better goal for a company is to maximize customer happiness divided by production cost. The higher this ratio is compared to the same ratio of a company's competitors, the more profit a company will make.

10. Ironically, maximum profit comes not from maximizing profit, but from maximizing customer happiness divided by production cost (H/C).

Natural history

When our world was created, it was imbued with the principle of *the survival of the fittest*. It was also imbued with the principle of *the fitness of the whole is greater than the sum of the fitness of the parts*. Guided by these two principles, life evolved "upward" toward ever better organisms and teams. Bacteria combined into cells, cells combined into plants and animals, and animals combined into hives, schools, flocks, herds, and packs. Random mutations that led to better groups survived; those that led to worse groups disappeared.

Human history

We humans continued, and continue, upward evolution. We invented tribes and chiefs, then agriculture, villages, cities, kingdoms, and empires, then industry, nations, and presidents.

Religions that lead us closer to a balance of strength, meekness, punishment, forgiveness, thrift and charity thrive (with the societies they support). Religions that lead us toward belligerence and revenge, or toward defensive weakness and tolerance of wrong, or toward debt, wither (with the societies they support).

Legal incorporation and stock markets are inventions that greatly aided the formation of businesses – the current epitome of worth-generating teams.

Each culture's list of heroes – kings, religious figures, inventors, culture shapers, generals, and recently business tycoons – traces the path of that culture's increase in team worth.

In summary:

11. History is the story of the evolution of increasingly synergistic organisms and teams, due to the interworking principles of "the survival of the fittest" and "the fitness of the whole is greater than the sum of the fitness of the parts".

Reverse teams

Democratic cities, states, and nations (and clubs and cooperatives, too) are teams of a special sort. They are *reverse teams*. A business pays team members for providing services to the business. In a reverse team such as a nation, however, team members pay the team for providing services to the team members.

Reverse teams create worth, or they wouldn't exist. They create worth directly and indirectly.

Directly, reverse teams use economy of scale to provide services to team members at a cost less than the cost team members would pay separately for the services. For example, all the citizens in a town pool tax money and buy new roads for $1 million. If the total price would have been $1.5 million if each citizen built their own section of road, $500,000 of worth is created by the town. Cooperatives also work on this principle.

Indirectly, reverse teams provide a framework within which businesses and individuals can operate more efficiently, therefore generating more worth for themselves. Inter-business teams, and even businesses themselves, must operate within some framework of laws and processes. Cities, states, and nations provide such frameworks. A portion of the worth created within the frameworks is taxed to operate the government; the rest is kept by the companies. Again, all parties gain.

In summary:

12. Reverse teams, such as cooperatives and democratic countries, create worth directly through economies of scale, and indirectly by providing a framework in which other teams can create worth. They are financed by a tax on a portion of the created worth.

Trade deficit

Running a trade deficit is not bad in itself. Both countries gain worth in every non-forced trade. It is what a country does with the created worth that determines winners and losers.

13. A trade deficit is not bad in itself. All countries gain worth from trading. The country that best reinvests its trade gains in new worth-generating capital is the country that wins, regardless of the direction of money flow.

Evolving economic ideas

Adam Smith (1723-1790)
The Wealth of Nations, Book I

Chapter I
The greatest improvement in the productive powers of labour ... seem to have been the effects of the division of labour.

Chapter II
It is not from the benevolence of the butcher, the brewer, or the baker, that we expect our dinner, but from their regard to their own interest.

Adam Smith published 'The Wealth of Nations' in 1776, the same year the American Declaration of Independence was signed.

David Ricardo (1772-1823)
Principles of Political Economy and Taxation

Chapter VII
Though she [Portugal] could make the cloth with the labour of 90 men, she would import it from a country [England] where it required the labour of 100 men to produce it, because it would be advantageous to her rather to employ her capital in the production of wine, for which she would obtain more cloth from England, than she could produce by diverting a portion of her capital from the cultivation of vines to the manufacture of cloth.

Ricardo's (often misinterpreted) law of comparative advantage says a country benefits most from specializing in what it does best relative to itself, not in what it does better than the countries it trades with.

Karl Marx (1818-1883)
Value, Price, And Profit: An Introduction to the Theory of Capitalism

Chapter VI. Value and Labor
Yet, *its [a commodity's] value remaining always the same*, ... it must be something distinct from, and independent of, these *different rates of exchange* with different articles.

If we consider *commodities as values*, we consider them exclusively under the single aspect of *realized, fixed*, or, if you like, *crystallized social labor*. ... But how does one measure *quantities of labor*? By the *time the labor lasts*, in measuring the labor by the hour, the day, etc.

Chapter X. Profit is made by Selling a Commodity at its Value
The value of a commodity is determined by the *total quantity of labor* contained in it. ... Part of the labor contained in the commodity is *paid* labor; part is *unpaid* labor. By selling, therefore, the commodity *at its value*, that is, as the crystallization of the *total quantity of labor* bestowed upon it, the capitalist must necessarily sell it at a profit. He sells not only what has cost him an equivalent, but he sells also what has cost him nothing, although it has cost his workman labor. ... I repeat, therefore, that normal and average profits are made by selling commodities not *above*, but *at their real values*.

Chapter XIV. The Struggle between Capital and Labor and its Results
Trades Unions work well as centers of resistance against the encroachments of capital. They fail partially from an injudicious use of their power. They fail generally from limiting themselves to a guerrilla war against the effects of the existing system, instead of simultaneously trying to change it,

instead of using their organized forces as a lever for the final emancipation of the working class, that is to say, the ultimate abolition of the wage system.

Karl Marx believed a commodity's value derives from man-hours. We agree. However, we assert that Karl Marx's belief that each commodity and man-hour has a single value (instead of changing its value with a change of ownership) led him to the misguided conclusion that profit derives only from the difference between a worker's output and his wages. This conclusion, in turn, led to a further miscalculation of the benefit of the emancipation of workers.

William Vickrey (1914-1996)

Vickrey showed that Dutch descending-price open-bid auctions, and sealed-bid auctions in which the winner pays the price that was bid, are equivalent. He also showed that English ascending-price open-bid auctions, and sealed-bid auctions in which the winner pays the second-highest price that was bid (called Vickrey auctions), are equivalent.

Though auctions are not the topic of this chapter, Vickrey's ideas are enlightening. The idea that the person who places the highest value on an item need pay only one dollar more than the amount the person who places the second-highest value on the item is willing to pay is an important part of understanding the creation of worth.

John Nash (1928-2015)

John Nash shared the 1994 Nobel Prize in Economic Sciences for his "pioneering analysis of equilibria in the theory of non-cooperative games".

We interpret Nash's work as showing that the benefits to society of Adam Smith's "invisible hand" of self-interest can become stuck at local maximi, and that cooperation is needed to move beyond these so-called Nash equilibria.

Thus, for society to benefit most, competition and cooperation must co-exist. For example, modern economic competition is bounded by rules we all agree on. No violence, no stealing, no cheating, no lying. If enough of us start breaking these rules, all of us must adversely adjust our behavior out of self-interest, collectively sinking to a lower Nash equilibrium, to the detriment of society.

S23.14 – Religion

(detail of) The Creation of Adam
(1512, fresco)

Michelangelo di Lodovico Buonarroti Simoni
(1475-1564), Italian painter, sculptor, architect.

In the beginning was the Word, and the Word was with God, and the Word was God.

John 1:1, King James Bible.

It is true, that a little Philosophy inclineth Man's Mind to Atheism; But depth in Philosophy, bringeth Men's Minds about to Religion.
Francis Bacon (1561-1626), English renaissance author, statesman, philosopher.

A little learning is a dangerous thing;
Drink deep, or taste not the Pierian spring;
There shallow draughts intoxicate the brain,
And drinking largely sobers us again.
Alexander Pope (1688- 1744) English poet, translator, and satirist.

For science can only ascertain what is, but not what should be, and outside of its domain value judgments of all kinds remain necessary.
Albert Einstein (1879-1955), German-born American physicist.

Does God exist?
Yes. Absolutely. Without a doubt.

God the creator created evolution. Evolution created ant colonies that need a queen to keep from disintegrating, created packs and herds that need a dominant animal to keep from disintegrating, and created human civilizations that need a shared belief in God to keep from disintegrating. The evolutionary leap from ape to man could not have happened without belief in God.

Did God create man, or did man create God?
This is a more nuanced question.

Before photography, artists became better and better over the years at capturing reality in stone and on canvas. These artists had full control over the stone and the canvas, but they had no control over the reality they were trying to depict. Therefore, the look of their sculptures and paintings became ever more life-like.

Similarly, even though humans have full control over religion, if a society wants to thrive, their religion must conform to the true nature of God. Consequently, humans have no control over the fact that religions move ever closer to a true understanding of God.

For society to function, each parent must imbue in their children their own personal understanding of God. The descendants of parents that convey a better understanding God flourish. The descendants of parents that convey a poorer understanding of God fall by the wayside.

Is my religion better than your religion? (historically)

Historically, the answer to this question was "yes" for everybody, accompanied by intolerance of other religions. One's own tribe's religion was part of their "us" identity, and the other tribe's religion was part of their "them" identity. The us vs them dynamic accompanied by intolerance contributed to the open warfare that was historically a normal part of existence.

In *The Histories* (3:38) Ancient Greek historian and geographer **Herodotus** (484 BC – 425 BC) observes on the relativity of customs:

> If anyone, no matter who, were given the opportunity of choosing from amongst all the nations in the world the set of beliefs which he thought best, he would inevitably—after careful considerations of their relative merits—choose that of his own country. Everyone without exception believes his own native customs, and the religion he was brought up in, to be the best.; and

that being so, it is unlikely that anyone but a madman would mock at such things. There is abundant evidence that this is the universal feeling about the ancient customs of one's country.

Is my religion better than your religion? (now)
S23 firmly believes the modern answer to this question is still "yes" for everybody, but a "yes" that is now accompanied by tolerance for other religions.

Religion used to be a football game – you won by advancing your own team and holding back the other team. Religion is now a foot race – you win by advancing your own team and not holding back the other team – holding back the other team is now against the rules.

Do religions improve?
Yes, but awkwardly. To improve, religions must overcome a difficult tension between short-term and long-term success. To work best in the short term, religions deliver an immutable truth from a power higher than man. To work best in the long term, religions move ever closer to a true understanding of God.

Protestant Christianity partially solves this tension by having a fixed Bible, and periodically forming new denominations. Judaism partially solves this tension by having a fixed Torah and an evolving interpretation of the Torah.

Should we strive for world peace?
If we look at religion over the years, the message about enemies is "love and forgive your enemies" rather than "do not have enemies". At this time in history, S23 posits that "civil competition" or "peaceful competition" is what we should strive for, rather than "no competition".

What are examples of civil competition?
Indian lawyer and anti-colonial nationalist **Mahatma Gandhi** (1869 – 1948) kept the moral high ground and used civil means to "struggle" against British occupation.

American minister and civil rights leader **Martin Luther King Jr.** (1929 – 1968) kept the moral high ground and used civil means to "struggle" against legal segregation.

South African anti-apartheid political leader **Nelson Mandela** (1918 – 2013) kept the moral high ground and used civil means to "struggle" against legal apartheid.

In the above cases, mature adults prevented real and serious struggles from degenerating into open warfare. And they did it without capitulating.

This bears repeating – adult diplomats solved difficult problems without warfare and without capitulation.

Living in oceans gave us our skeletons, living in trees gave us our dexterous hands, and open warfare developed our wonderful brains. But the time for living in oceans, the time for living in trees, and the time for beneficial open warfare has passed.

Will the meek inherit the Earth?
Yes. Meek adults – those who avoid provoking others, avoid hate and revenge, but *also avoid capitulation* – will win.

In summary
Between a society with religion and a society without religion, the society with religion wins.

Between two societies with religion, the society whose religion comes closest to capturing the true essence of God wins.

Without God, a society cannot maintain moral power. It cannot both love its enemies and stand up to its enemies – it will either start hating or it will capitulate.

S23.15 – Social Structure

The Naval Battle of Corinth
(1630, copper engraving)

***Matthäus Merian the Elder** (1593 – 1650), Swiss-born engraver and publisher.*

(Naval victory for Athens over the fleet of Sparta and Corinth, 430 BC, during the Peloponnesian War)

A society perpetuates itself by passing down from parent to children the contents of the brain's religion, language, and culture receptacles. This inherited content causes individuals to act in such a way that each aggregate society has a unique structure.

Just as genes mutate when passed from parent to child, so too do religion, language, and culture. Consequently, social structure evolves.

If there were one best social structure for winning wars, all societies would smoothly evolve toward it.

Instead, there are several different social structures that contribute to winning wars, each with strengths and weaknesses. Think Sparta and Athens.

These competing strengths and weaknesses create an evolutionary tension between social structures. In the long term, social progress is achieved, but the progress is slow and uneven.

Three social structures that help win wars are:

- Authoritarian (a hierarchy of leaders and followers),
- Nash/Smith (Old Testament), and
- Nash/Smith (New Testament)

A hierarchy of leaders

When actually fighting a war, or when a poor nation is trying to catch up to a rich nation, a recursive hierarchy of leaders and followers is the best social structure. One example is a modern army with generals, colonels, captains, sergeants, and privates. Another example is feudal Europe, with kings, dukes, earls, squires, and peasants.

Nash/Smith

For producing wealth in an advanced nation, however, the best social structure is something S23 calls a Nash/Smith social structure. In a Nash/Smith society, all citizens believe in, and obey, a common set of rules and customs. For example, don't murder, don't steal, and honor signed contracts. Within this common set of rules and customs, each citizen pursues their own self-interest.

Scottish economist and philosopher **Adam Smith** (1723 – 1790) labeled the fact that a society benefits when each citizen pursues their own self-interest the *invisible hand*. American mathematician **John Forbes Nash Jr.** (1928 – 2015) won the Nobel Memorial Prize in Economic Sciences in 1994 for showing that different levels of cooperation are needed for the invisible hand to work at different levels of benefit.

Single visible goal vs. exploration

Another way of explaining the strengths and weaknesses of government types is the following.

An authoritarian government (with top-down leadership) works best when a nation has a single visible goal – when the nation is being attacked or when it is trying to catch up to a richer neighbor.

A Nash/Smith society (where the government provides rules and then gets out of the way) works best when an advanced nation is exploring new opportunities to create wealth. Governments are good at winning wars and bad at exploring; self-interested people are bad at winning wars and good at exploring.

Cheater's paradox

If everybody in a Nash/Smith society follows the rules, everybody benefits. If everybody follows the rules except one person who cheats, everybody benefits, but the cheater benefits most. If enough people cheat, everybody suffers, including the cheaters.

To allow humans to form a Nash/Smith society, evolution had to develop a way to discourage cheaters from cheating.

Shame, indignation, and the desire to punish

Shame is an instinctive emotional reaction to you breaking one of the rules that is programmed into one of *your* brain receptacles. For example, try saying the sentence "Sentence this purple ain't grammar good.", or try walking down the street in ridiculous looking clothes.

Indignation is an instinctive emotional reaction to someone else breaking a rule you feel should be programmed into one of *their* brain receptacles. The emotional *desire to punish* and *desire for revenge* are stronger versions of indignation.

Personal shame and the threat of punishment and revenge from others combine as one way to discourage cheaters from cheating.

Agape

If a society's religion comes close enough to a true understanding of God, there is an alternative emotion that can be used to discouraging cheating, or, more accurately, encourage non-cheating. That is the emotion of love. Specifically of ***agape*** – an unconditional love of all people.

Agape is not the absence of punishment; it is reluctant punishment that stems from a desire to improve – punishment without the *desire* to punish. After necessary punishment, agape is forgiveness.

Nash/Smith (Old Testament)
S23 labels a Nash/Smith society that discourages cheaters using the threat of punishment and revenge a *Nash/Smith (Old Testament)* society.

Nash/Smith (New Testament)
S23 labels a Nash/Smith society that encourages non-cheating using agape a *Nash/Smith (New Testament)* society.

The terms "Old Testament" and "New Testament" come from Christianity, but any modern religion can support either type of society.

Nash/Smith (New Testament) societies are richer and harder to maintain; Nash/Smith (Old Testament) societies are poorer and easier to maintain.

The world in the twenty-first century
In the twentieth century, the economic system of free-market capitalism triumphed over the economic system of communism. All successful societies in the twenty-first century employ free-market capitalism.

The struggle in this century is between:

- single-party capitalism (de jure),
- single-party capitalism (de facto),
- two-party liberal democratic capitalism, and
- multi-party liberal democratic capitalism.

Which of these systems is best for mankind?
For an individual, their own form of society is best. For mankind, at this point in time, having all four social systems, and having them compete (without open warfare), is best.

S23.16 – Collecting Seashells

A Learning Hectosophy

Shiohigari (Gathering Shells)
(1810s, color woodblock print)

Utagawa, Kunitora *(1789 - 1868), Japanese artist.*

Chapter contents

This chapter contains a collection of learning aphorisms. It is an early version of the author's philosophy, collected mostly between 1995 and 2010.

The author's first philosophy book was published in 2016. If the philosophy of this chapter is called S10, and the philosophy of the author's first book is called S16, then the progression of S10, S16, and S23 illustrates the evolving nature of know-how philosophy.

For meta-arks that copy the structure of S23, but have no need of showing a historical progression, this chapter represents a catch-all chapter – a place to add learning insights and observations that do not fit in other chapters.

Collecting seashells

Three seashell collectors spent the summer at a beach.

The first collector carried a basket that held ten shells. Each day she collected ten pretty shells in her basket. She took them home and displayed them. At the end of the summer she had hundreds of pretty shells.

The second collector carried a basket that held ten shells. He spent two weeks collecting ten very pretty shells in his basket. He took them home and displayed them. He spent the rest of the summer fishing. At the end of the summer he had ten very pretty shells.

The third collector carried a basket that held ten shells. Each day she collected ten pretty shells in her basket. She took them home. Of her existing and new shells, she kept the ten prettiest, and displayed them. At the end of the summer she had ten gorgeous shells.

Some secrets

The disciple trudged across the remote Tibetan valley and slowly pulled himself up the steep cliff. He caught his breath, knocked on the monastery door, and asked the wizened monk who answered: "Master, may I ask you a question?" The monk slowly nodded.

"What is 'the secret' of wisdom?" the disciple asked. The monk smiled and replied, "One secret of wisdom is to think plural, not singular."

The disciple smiled. "Well, then. What are 'the secrets' of wisdom?" The monk smiled and replied, "One secret of wisdom is to think partial, not final."

The disciple smiled. "Well, then. What are 'some secrets' of wisdom?" The monk smiled. The disciple smiled. "Thank you," the disciple said.

The genie of skills

A young woman saw a lamp washed up on the beach. She polished it. The face of a genie appeared in the air before her.

"I am the Genie of Skills," the genie said. "I was trapped in this lamp by my enemies. If you follow my instructions and let me out, I will grant you expertise in one skill."

The young woman said to the genie "Please let me think a minute".

She pictured herself as an expert figure skater, an expert actress, an expert businesswoman, an expert mother, an expert lawyer, an expert teacher, and an expert politician.

She then replied to the genie "Yes, I will let you out, if, in return, you grant me expertise in the skill of acquiring expertise".

Long division contest

The math contest judge looked sternly down at the girl. "What is 70 divided by ten?" asked the judge. "Seven," replied the girl. "What is 71 divided by ten?" asked the judge. "Seven point one," replied the girl.

"Hmmm," intoned the judge, concentrating, "What is an iron bar divided by ten?". "Ten iron pieces," replied the girl. "What is an iron smelting process divided by ten?" asked the judge. "Ten iron process steps," replied the girl.

"And what is the skill of blacksmithing divided by ten?" the judge asked smugly. The girl pondered for a moment. "Ten iron skillets?" she ventured. She won the contest.

Record what worked
To learn and improve, record what worked. In notebooks, on scraps of paper, or in computer documents.

Occasionally summarize
Occasionally summarize what worked into a decasophy or a hectosophy. Over time, this forces an increase in quality, not quantity.

Decasophies and Hectosophies
For convenience, the following words are defined:

decasophy (de kas' ə fee)
noun: A collection of ten subjective ideas, observations, practices, rules, or techniques. *From the Greek "deca" meaning ten, and "sophy" meaning knowledge or wisdom.*

hectosophy (hek tos' ə fee)
noun: A collection of one hundred subjective ideas, observations, practices, rules, or techniques. Sometimes composed of ten decasophies. *From the Greek "hecto" meaning one hundred, and "sophy" meaning knowledge or wisdom.*

Prithee a pithy appellation
Label ideas, observations, and practices with short, meaningful names.

The quickest route
Two men, each with an old car that could travel no faster than forty miles per hour, decided to drive to California from the East Coast. They would depart in one week.

The first man spent the week figuring out the shortest route to take. The second man spent the week fixing his car so it would travel faster than forty miles per hour.

Third grade student, fourth grade problem
A third grade student encountered a fourth grade problem. He pondered whether he should work hard trying to solve the problem using his third grade techniques, or put the problem aside, work hard at school, and tackle the problem when he reached the fourth grade, using fourth grade techniques.

Rise above it
You can't solve a problem on the same level that it was created. You have to rise above it to the next level.
***Albert Einstein** (1879-1955), German-born American physicist.*

Know-like-do-learn-know
If you know how to do something, you like it. If you like something, you do it. If you do something, you learn it. If you learn something, you know more about it.

This learning cycle is a positive feedback loop that has two states: *on* and *off*. You are either doing and learning, or not doing and not learning.

Machine gun approach
How do we start to learn? Or restart to learn? One way is to try anything and everything. Try one hundred small doable tasks, each vaguely related to what you want to learn.

One hundred near-random efforts will teach something. Use this knowledge to plan the next one hundred (hopefully less random) doable tasks. Eventually you will learn enough to progress in a systematic way. In other words: flail, ratchet, repeat.

The Scylla and Charybdis of learning
If you avoid the Scylla of not knowing how to learn, be wary of the Charybdis of knowing how to learn, having it be wrong, *and not changing it.*

You learn what you practice
If you practice swimming, you learn to swim. If you practice learning, you learn to learn. If you practice succeeding, you learn to succeed.

The way to succeed
The way to succeed is to double your failure rate.
Thomas J. Watson Sr. *(1874-1956), American businessman, founder of IBM.*

Failing to learn; learning to fail
To learn, you must conduct trial and error. Trial and error involves failure.

Since you learn what you practice, you face the very real danger of learning to fail as you attempt to learn something hard. As you try and try again to reach a difficult goal without success, your attempts become similar and halfhearted. You stop trying new things. You assume continual failure, and achieve continual failure.

Each day differently
Following rules written on paper slows trial and error, and thus learning. Do important things differently each day.

Wheel-spinner goal
A wheel-spinner goal is a goal that puts you into a try and fail loop, without making progress. Picture a car that is stuck. The

accelerator is repeatedly pressed. The car does not move. Instead, it digs itself deeper into a rut.

Pot-of-gold goal (aka byproduct goal)

Like the pot of gold at the end of the rainbow, there are some goals with built-in dynamics that make them wheel-spinner goals if they are pursued directly. Progress toward such goals is best made obliquely as a byproduct of pursuing other goals.

A wild animal will not eat out of your hand if you keep walking toward it. Maximizing a company's profits in the short term cannibalizes long-term value. Pleasing everybody cannibalizes long-term success and respect.

A wild animal must come to you. Profits come from satisfying customers. If you are honest, helpful, and successful, many people will like you.

Deciduous goal

A deciduous (baby-tooth) goal is a goal set by a beginning learner that is later discarded in favor of a better learning goal.

Wittgenstein's ladder

My propositions are elucidatory in this way: he who understands me finally recognizes them as senseless, when he has climbed out through them, on them, over them. (He must so to speak throw away the ladder, after he has climbed up on it.)
Ludwig Wittgenstein *(1889-1951), Austrian philosopher.*

It feels like one big secret

Expertise-based endeavors, such as software development, business, and getting along with others, are improved by learning many small insights.

However, when one does not know how to do such an endeavor, it feels as if one is missing one big secret, not many small insights.

In the process of learning these many small insights, one of them may cause an "ah-ha" or a "eureka". This small "breakthrough" insight feels like one big secret.

And when one eventually becomes good at something, and tries to explain it to others, it feels as if there is one big secret to explain, not many small insights.

These feelings are real. They are as strong in good learners as in beginning learners. Good learners, however, ignore these feelings better.

Faith in God.
Faith in me.
Faith in the little rules
I can't yet see.

Bad goal or bad me

Our to-do goals involve tasks with which we are familiar. Our learning goals, by definition, involve tasks we are less familiar with. If our progress toward a learning goal stalls, who or what is at fault?

Are we not smart enough? Are we not working hard enough? Or did we choose a poor goal?

It is the goal's fault

You *are* smart enough. You *are* working hard enough. It *is* the learning goal's fault.

Artificial experience

Speeding up learning often means speeding up the acquisition of experience. Three types of goals help.

- An *emotional goal* inspires and motivates.
- A *SALI (single axis of learning and improvement)* defines a component of a skill. Each SALI has a single clear definition of better.
- A short-term *practice goal* is designed to artificially maximize experience. A single practice goal can address a single SALI or multiple SALI's.

To be state basketball champions might be an inspiring goal for high school basketball players. Dribbling a basketball, shooting, defense, and running plays might be SALI's. A practice goal might be to play "follow the leader", and have basketball players follow a leader while dribbling basketballs.

Aim at Boston, measure from yesterday.

In mathematics, a vector is defined by a direction and a magnitude. Goals also comprise a direction and a magnitude.

When pursuing a difficult goal, it is often better to measure daily progress, or progress from the starting point, than to measure remaining distance. For example, if you set a goal of walking from San Francisco to Boston, use Boston to set direction, while measuring miles walked per day, or miles walked from San Francisco.

A doable equation

undoable = $\sum$ doable

As a compass needle
Aim at perfection as a compass needle aims at north.

Perfection is the
Long-term aim,
Completion is the
Short-term game.

You, too, can become great
Keep away from people who try to belittle your ambitions. Small people always do that, but the really great make you feel that you, too, can become great.
Mark Twain *(1835-1910), American writer, humorist.*

Be discouraged
"Don't be discouraged" is a hard rule to follow. Be discouraged. Wallow. For a while. Then become excited again.

No one can stop you
If you are not willing to learn, no one can help you. If you are determined to learn, no one can stop you.
Hilary "Zig" Ziglar *(1926 – 2012), American author and motivational speaker.*

Scientia potentia est
Knowledge is power.
(attributed to) ***Francis Bacon*** *(1561-1626), English renaissance author, statesman, philosopher.*

Grace

Knowledge is but folly unless it is guided by grace.
George Herbert, (1593-1633), Welsh-born English poet, orator, priest.

Courage

I learned that courage was not the absence of fear, but the triumph over it.
Nelson Mandela (1900-2013), South African politician.

Do it anyway

People are often unreasonable, irrational, and self-centered.
    Forgive them anyway.
If you are kind, people may accuse you of selfish, ulterior motives.
    Be kind anyway.
If you are successful, you will win some unfaithful friends and some genuine enemies.
    Succeed anyway.
If you are honest and sincere people may deceive you.
    Be honest and sincere anyway.
What you spend years creating, others could destroy overnight.
    Create anyway.
If you find serenity and happiness, some may be jealous.
    Be happy anyway.
The good you do today, will often be forgotten.
    Do good anyway.
Give the best you have, and it will never be enough.
    Give your best anyway.
In the final analysis, it is between you and God.
    It was never between you and them anyway.
Mother Teresa (1910-1997), Albanian-born Roman Catholic nun. Adapted from 'The Paradoxical Commandments' by Kent M. Keith (1949-), American author.

We should all be thankful
In everyone's life, at some time, our inner fire goes out. It is then burst into flame by an encounter with another human being. We should all be thankful for those people who rekindle the inner spirit.
***Albert Schweitzer** (1875-1965), Alsatian theologian.*

Twenty-five years after Darwin
The known is finite, the unknown infinite; intellectually we stand on an islet in the midst of an illimitable ocean of inexplicability. Our business in every generation is to reclaim a little more land, to add something to the extent and the solidity of our possessions. And even a cursory glance at the history of the biological sciences during the last quarter of a century is sufficient to justify the assertion, that the most potent instrument for the extension of the realm of natural knowledge which has come into men's hands, since the publication of Newton's 'Principia,' is Darwin's 'Origin of Species.'

It was badly received by the generation to which it was first addressed, and the outpouring of angry nonsense to which it gave rise is sad to think upon. But the present generation will probably behave just as badly if another Darwin should arise, and inflict upon them that which the generality of mankind most hate – the necessity of revising their convictions.
***Thomas Henry Huxley** (1825-1895), British biologist.*

Given with love
Whenever you have truth it must be given with love, or the message and the messenger will be rejected.
***Mahatma Gandhi** (1869-1948), Indian political and spiritual leader.*

Don't shoot the message
Don't shoot the message because of the messenger.

Put the map at the back

The king gave the famous explorer a partially completed map showing the known territory of his kingdom and asked him to explore the unknown territory.

While traveling through the known territory, the explorer put the map at the head of his column, and used it to navigate.

When he began to explore the unknown territory, he put the map at the back of his column, and used it to record where he had been.

Granny gear

The long-distance bicyclist pedaled at a constant pace. When he got to a hill, he down-shifted. His bike went slower, but not his pedaling. When he got to a steep hill, he down-shifted to his lowest gear, called "granny gear". And when even that gear was not low enough, he took a different route, still pedaling at his constant pace.

AAA

In addition to reducing a list to ten or one hundred items, another culling technique is to reduce a list until all items are of equal (high) value. In other words, keep the A's, and remove the B's and C's and D's. This approach is useful for culling material things, such as clothes in a closet or boxes in an attic.

A learner of distinction

Before the young man attended butcher school, meat was meat. As he became more adept at slicing meat, meat became beef, pork, chicken, and lamb. Beef became chuck, rib, short loin, sirloin, shank, brisket, plate, and flank. Short loin became top loin steak, T-bone steak, Porterhouse steak, tenderloin roast, and tenderloin steak. And each cut of beef came in prime, choice, and select quality grades.

One for all and all for one
In complex systems, each problem is partially addressed by many practices that work. And each practice that works partially addresses many problems. In other words, there is a many-to-many relationship between problems and practices.

This makes it hard to progress by fixing one problem at a time. Instead, focus on making improvements. As you gradually improve, you gradually chip away at all problems.

Happy families
Happy families are all alike; every unhappy family is unhappy in its own way.
Leo Tolstoy *(1828-1910), Russian author and philosopher.*

Fixing and solving are problematic. Better is better.

For or against
Strive *for*, rather than *against*.

The shift
The shift from fixing problems to steady improvement is a gradual one.

Aristotle's ideas about people
The young history student read an essay on Aristotle that stated Aristotle's ideas about physics had long been superseded, but his ideas about people were as relevant today as they were 2500 years ago. At first, she smiled in agreement – after all, people had not changed in 2500 years.

But on deeper reflection, she was puzzled. Just as people had not changed in 2500 years, neither had the laws of nature.

Snowballs

Record what worked for recording what worked.
Learn the skill of learning skills.
Develop the habit of developing good habits.
Learn from others how to learn from others.

Love to learn
To love to learn

Beware the urge

When recording what worked:
    Beware the urge for correctness.
    Beware the urge for completeness.
    Beware the urge for consistency.
    Watch out for the desire to fit things into patterns.

A collection of what worked is messy, incomplete, and contradictory.

Very well then

Do I contradict myself? Very well then I contradict myself. I am large, I contain multitudes.
Walt Whitman *(1819-1892), American poet.*

Simple Pragmatism and Pure Elegance

Simple Pragmatism is the plain and hard-working little sister of the beautiful and alluring Pure Elegance. If you marry Simple Pragmatism, be careful. Since Simple Pragmatism and Pure Elegance are related, Pure Elegance will be seductively near. It is OK to admire her, and even desire her, but you must never embrace her. If Simple Pragmatism catches you in the arms of Pure Elegance, she will divorce you.

Single ideas
Beware the urge to analyze single subjective ideas. All subjective ideas have flaws and merits, and are better analyzed by comparing them to other subjective ideas.

Improvement tax
During each time interval or task, use some percentage of time for improvement. Improve your environment, tools, and techniques. Record what worked.

Riding a half-tamed horse
Sometimes it seems we are five percent rational beings and ninety-five percent habitual beings. As if we are in charge of ourselves the same way a rider is in charge of a half-tamed horse.

Excellence
If you want to achieve excellence, you can get there today. As of this second, quit doing less-than-excellent work.
Thomas J. Watson Sr. *(1874-1956), American businessman, founder of IBM.*

Acquire quality
Men acquire a particular quality by constantly acting a particular way...you become just by performing just actions, temperate by performing temperate actions, brave by performing brave actions.
Aristotle *(384-322 BC), Greek philosopher.*

Agreeable

Choose the life that is most useful, and habit will make it the most agreeable.
Francis Bacon (1561-1626), English renaissance author, statesman, philosopher.

Francis Bacon

Bacon left a heritage to English science. His writings and his thoughts are not always clear, but he firmly held, and, with the authority which his personal eminence gave him, firmly proclaimed, that the careful and systematic investigation of natural phenomena and their accurate record would give to man a power in this world which, in his time, was hardly to be conceived.

He did more than anyone else to help to free the intellect from preconceived notions and to direct it to the unbiased study of facts, whether of nature, of mind, or of society; he vindicated an independent position for the positive sciences; and to this, in the main, he owes his position in the history of modern thought.

Though Bacon did not make any one single advance in natural knowledge – though his precepts, as Whewell reminds us, "are now practically useless" – yet he used his great talents, his high position, to enforce upon the world a new method of wrenching from nature her secrets and, with tireless patience and untiring passion, impressed upon his contemporaries the conviction that there was "a new unexplored Kingdom of Knowledge within the reach and grasp of man, if he will be humble enough, and patient enough, and truthful enough to occupy it."

The Cambridge history of English and American literature, ed. by A.W. Ward et al., New York: G.P. Putnam's Sons; Cambridge: University Press, 1907-21

The idea of progress
Though it is hard to pinpoint the birth of an idea, for all intents and purposes the modern idea of technological "progress" (in the sense of a steady, cumulative, historical advance in applied scientific knowledge) began with Bacon's *The Advancement of Learning* and became fully articulated in his later works.

That history might in fact be progressive, i.e., an onward and upward ascent – and not, as Aristotle had taught, merely cyclical or, as cultural pessimists from Hesiod to Spengler have supposed, a descending or retrograde movement – became for Bacon an article of secular faith which he propounded with evangelical force and a sense of mission. In the Advancement, the idea is offered tentatively, as a kind of hopeful hypothesis. But in later works such as the New Organon, it becomes almost a promised destiny: Enlightenment and a better world, Bacon insists, lie within our power; they require only the cooperation of learned citizens and the active development of the arts and sciences.
The Internet Encyclopedia of Philosophy
http://www.iep.utm.edu/b/bacon.htm (03/26/2014).

Sharing subjective theories
Influenced by the amazing power of the scientific method coupled with peer-reviewed journals, we often attempt to share subjective ideas the same way we share natural-science ideas: as single theories, supported by rational arguments.

Single theories and reproducible experiments are the bricks of which science is built. Unfortunately, single theories seem of less value when sharing subjective ideas.

Without the backing of repeatable experiments, people quibble over them. Even worse than complete rejection, single subjective theories lead to partial agreement. If one author agrees with eighty percent of another author's theory, she must propose a new theory to express her viewpoint. The result is two competing theories with a small difference.

Is there a better format?

Is there a better format than single theories for sharing subjective ideas? A format that better allows us to disagree with, learn from, and add to each other's views?

Comparing boxes of apples and boxes of apples

The judge walked among the apple stands at the county fair. One stand displayed three big apples. Another displayed a basket of apples decorated with flowers. Yet another stand displayed a pyramid of fifty-five apples.

"How can I fairly compare these displays?" the judge asked himself.

He had an idea. He gave each stand an identical box that held ten apples. "Put your ten best apples in this box," he said, "and I will select the stand with the best box".

Combining boxes of apples

The state fair was one week later. Instead of entering the box of apples that had won first prize at the county fair, the apple stand owners decided to combine their boxes. They created a new box, with the ten best apples from the existing boxes, and entered the new box at the state fair.

Theory

Theory is a friend of science, and a subtle enemy of philosophy.

Consensus

Consensus is a friend of joint action, and a subtle enemy of joint learning.

Observation
Observation is a friend of everybody.

Subjective group research – to each his own
Hectosophies signed by multiple authors are not useful. When Tommy's group researches a subjective topic, each person in the group produces his or her own hectosophy.

Subjective group action – consensus is needed
Groups designed for action need rules and processes. When Tina's group works on a project, they jointly agree on rules and processes to follow during the project.

A vision
A vision... Experts are convened in a room, discussing a subjective topic. Each presents ten ideas that work for him or her. There are questions, but no debate.

The experts adjourn to modify their presentations, based on what they learned from each other. They reconvene to each present their revised sets of ten ideas, then socialize and go home, each a little wiser.

The humanities, of course
A humanities course is designed to expose students to a subjective topic. It presents to students many opinions, then requires them to form and articulate their own opinion by writing papers and discoursing in class.

A humanities course that taught learning might be a powerful course. Learning opinions and case studies could be presented to students, who would be required to form their own opinion of learning by discoursing in class and recording what personally has worked for them.

L' Envoi

When Earth's last picture is painted and the tubes are twisted and dried,
When the oldest colours have faded, and the youngest critic has died,
We shall rest, and, faith, we shall need it -- lie down for an aeon or two,
Till the Master of All Good Workmen shall put us to work anew!

And those that were good shall be happy: they shall sit in a golden chair;
They shall splash at a ten-league canvas with brushes of comets' hair;
They shall find real saints to draw from -- Magdalene, Peter, and Paul;
They shall work for an age at a sitting and never be tired at all!

And only the Master shall praise us, and only the Master shall blame;
And no one shall work for money, and no one shall work for fame,
But each for the joy of the working, and each, in his separate star,
Shall draw the Thing as he sees It for the God of things as they are!
Rudyard Kipling *(1865-1936), British author, poet.*

A dark and stormy night

It was a dark and stormy night. Fred Ranck (Ph.D., mathematics) walked briskly out of the set theory conference in the "Mediterranean" room of the big uptown hotel, and hurried down the corridor, clutching his PowerPoint slides and Mountain Dew cola. Susan Tyne (Ph.D., philosophy) wandered slowly out of the history of philosophy seminar in the "Aegean" room of the same hotel, balancing 84 index-carded notes on how Darwin's theory of evolution affected philosophy, and one Starbucks coffee.

She paused at the corner, her eyes absently noting the wave-like patterns of the corridor lights on the long expanse of blue-green carpet, deep in thought about philosophy and evolution. He barreled around the corner. Lighting flashed, thunder bashed. Researchers crashed, coffee and cola splashed. Slides and cards were mashed in a heap on the floor.

"You got philosophy and coffee on my set theory!" yelped the mathematician.

"You got set theory and cola in my philosophy!" exclaimed the philosopher.

They looked down. The pile wriggled and writhed. Suddenly what looked like a brown and yellow origami centipede slithered from under the papers.

"Wh-What are you?" gulped Dr. Fred Ranck.

"I am a sophy-set," said the creature, matter-of-factly.

"Wh-What do you want?" stammered Dr. Susan Tyne.

"I want to find a sophy-set of the opposite gender," chuckled the sophy-set.

"Wh-Why?" mumbled Drs. F. Ranck and S. Tyne together.

"Why do you think?" chortled the sophy-set. "I want to make baby sophy-sets."

Improving improvement

Learning to speak accelerated human improvement. Writing accelerated human improvement. Printing accelerated human improvement. The invention of Western science accelerated human improvement. The development of formal process improvement and quality improvement in the mid-1900s accelerated human improvement.

The following Wikipedia articles about quality improvement are of interest.

Training Within Industry

http://en.wikipedia.org/wiki/Training_Within_Industry (05/27/2022).

The Training Within Industry (TWI) service was created by the United States Department of War, running from 1940 to 1945 within the War Manpower Commission. The purpose was to provide consulting services to war-related industries whose personnel were being conscripted into the US Army at the same time the War Department was issuing orders for additional matériel. It was apparent that the shortage of trained and skilled personnel at precisely the time they were needed most would impose a hardship on those industries, and that only improved methods of job training would address the shortfall.[1] By the end of World War II, over 1.6 million workers in over 16,500 plants had received a certification.

…Although the TWI program funding for application of the programs in the USA by the government ended in 1945, the US government did fund the introduction to the war-torn nations of Europe and Asia. … It was especially well received in Japan, where TWI formed the basis of the kaizen culture in industry. Kaizen, known by such names as Quality Circles in the West, was successfully harnessed by Toyota Motor Corporation in conjunction with the Lean or Just In Time principles of Taiichi

Ohno. In the foreword to Dinero's book "Training Within Industry", John Shook relates a story in which a Toyota trainer brought out an old copy of a TWI service manual to prove to him that American workers at NUMMI could be taught using the "Japanese" methods used at Toyota. Thus, TWI was the forerunner of what is today regarded as a Japanese creation.

Walter A. Shewhart

http://en.wikipedia.org/wiki/Shewhart (05/30/2022).

Walter Andrew Shewhart (1891-1967) was an American physicist, engineer and statistician, sometimes known as the father of statistical quality control.

…When Dr. Shewhart joined the Western Electric Company Inspection Engineering Department at the Hawthorne Works in 1918, industrial quality was limited to inspecting finished products and removing defective items. That all changed on May 16, 1924. Dr. Shewhart's boss, George D. Edwards, recalled: "Dr. Shewhart prepared a little memorandum only about a page in length. About a third of that page was given over to a simple diagram which we would all recognize today as a schematic control chart. That diagram, and the short text which preceded and followed it, set forth all of the essential principles and considerations which are involved in what we know today as process quality control."

…In 1938 his work came to the attention of physicists W. Edwards Deming and Raymond T. Birge.

…The encounter began a long collaboration between Shewhart and Deming that involved work on productivity during World War II and Deming's championing of Shewhart's ideas in Japan from 1950 onwards. Deming developed some of Shewhart's methodological proposals around scientific inference and named his synthesis the Shewhart cycle that later became the PDSA cycle.

W. Edwards Deming

http://en.wikipedia.org/wiki/Edward_Deming (05/30/2022).

William Edwards Deming (October 14, 1900-December 20, 1993) was an American engineer, statistician, professor, author, lecturer, and management consultant.

…In 1947, Deming was involved in early planning for the 1951 Japanese Census. The Allied powers were occupying Japan, and he was asked by the United States Department of the Army to assist with the census. He was brought over at the behest of General Douglas MacArthur, who grew frustrated at being unable to complete so much as a phone call without the line going dead due to Japans shattered post-war economy. While in Japan, his expertise in quality control techniques, combined with his involvement in Japanese society, brought him an invitation from the Japanese Union of Scientists and Engineers (JUSE).

JUSE members had studied Shewhart's techniques, and as part of Japan's reconstruction efforts, they sought an expert to teach statistical control. From June–August 1950, Deming trained hundreds of engineers, managers, and scholars in statistical process control (SPC) and concepts of quality. He also conducted at least one session for top management (including top Japanese industrialists of the likes of Akio Morita, the cofounder of Sony Corp.) Deming's message to Japan's chief executives was that improving quality would reduce expenses while increasing productivity and market share. Perhaps the best known of these management lectures was delivered at the Mt. Hakone Conference Center in August 1950.

A number of Japanese manufacturers applied his techniques widely and experienced heretofore unheard-of levels of quality and productivity. The improved quality combined with the lowered cost created new international demand for Japanese products.

Plan–Do–Check–Act Cycle
http://en.wikipedia.org/wiki/PDCA (05/30/2022).

PDCA (plan–do–check–act or plan–do–check–adjust) is an iterative design and management method used in business for the control and continual improvement of processes and products. It is also known as the Deming circle/cycle/wheel, the Shewhart cycle, the control circle/cycle, or plan–do–study–act (PDSA).

…PDCA is associated with W. Edwards Deming, who is considered by many to be the father of modern quality control; however, he … referred to it as the "Shewhart cycle". Later in Deming's career, he modified PDCA to "Plan, Do, Study, Act" (PDSA) because he felt that "check" emphasized inspection over analysis

S23.17 – Summary

Britannia between Scylla and Charybdis, or The Vessel of the Constitution steered clear of the Rock of Democracy, and the Whirlpool of Arbitrary-Power
(1793, engraving, political cartoon)

James Gillray (1756-1815), British caricaturist and printmaker.

There is no experience from which you can't learn something. When you stop learning you stop living in any vital and meaningful sense. And the purpose of life, after all, is to live it, to taste experience to the utmost, to reach out eagerly and without fear for newer and richer experience...
Eleanor Roosevelt (1884 – 1962), American first lady and diplomat.

God created humans by improvement, for improvement.

The individual who best integrates God, science, judgement, and self-improvement wins.

The learning team with the best rules (that support co-improvement) wins.

A mean team will defeat a same-sized nice team; a nice team will have more members.

Societies with bounded competition are richer than societies with no bounds (law of the jungle), and societies with no competition (communes).

The society that best integrates God, science, judgement, and collective improvement (to create a large team of nice people engaged in well-bounded competition) wins.

I love to win,
I love to lose,
The grandest fun
Is to improve.

Ever tried. Ever failed. No matter. Try Again. Fail again. Fail better.
Samuel Beckett *(1906-1989), Irish playwright, novelist.*

I believe that man will not merely endure: he will prevail. He is immortal, not because he alone among creatures has an inexhaustible voice, but because he has a soul, a spirit capable of compassion and sacrifice and endurance.
William Faulkner *(1897-1962), American author.*

Knowledge for the sake of understanding, not merely to prevail, that is the essence of our being. None can define its limits, or set its ultimate boundaries.
Vannevar Bush *(1890-1974), American engineer, inventor.*

The difference between what we do and what we are capable of doing would suffice to solve most of the world's problems.
Mahatma Gandhi *(1869-1948), Indian political and spiritual leader.*

Never give in, never give in, never; never; never; never – in nothing, great or small, large or petty – never give in except to convictions of honor and good sense.
Winston Churchill *(1874-1965), British statesman, author.*

The Author

Stan Silver worked thirty years as a software developer. He served as a captain in the U.S. Army, and has a master's degree in aerospace engineering, with a concentration in feedback control theory.

His focus shifted to philosophy and subjective learning when, after several years as a software developer, he realized he had no idea how to systematically improve software development.

author@knowhowphilosophy.com

www.ingramcontent.com/pod-product-compliance
Lightning Source LLC
Chambersburg PA
CBHW051104160426
43193CB00010B/1306